C

Economic
Integration
in New
Communities

New Communities Research Series

Shirley F. Weiss and *Raymond J. Burby, III*, series editors
Center for Urban and Regional Studies,
The University of North Carolina at Chapel Hill

- Access, Travel, and Transportation in New Communities by Robert B. Zehner

- Economic Integration in New Communities: An Evaluation of Factors Affecting Policies and Implementation by Helene V. Smookler

- Health Care in New Communities by Norman H. Loewenthal and Raymond J. Burby, III

- Indicators of the Quality of Life in New Communities by Robert B. Zehner

- Recreation and Leisure in New Communities by Raymond J. Burby, III

- Residential Mobility in New Communities: An Analysis of Recent In-movers and Prospective Out-movers by Edward J. Kaiser

- Schools in New Communities by Raymond J. Burby, III and Thomas G. Donnelly

Economic Integration in New Communities

An Evaluation of Factors Affecting Policies and Implemention

Helene V. Smookler

Ballinger Publishing Company • Cambridge, Massachusetts
A Subsidiary of J.B. Lippincott Company

This book is printed on recycled paper.

NSF–RA–E'75–029

All of the material incorporated in this work was developed with the support of National Science Foundation grant number APR 72–03425. However, any opinions, findings, conclusions or recommendations expressed herein are those of the author and do not necessarily reflect the views of the National Science Foundation.

International Standard Book Number: 0–88410–457–5

Library of Congress Catalog Card Number: 76–18298

Printed in the United States of America

Library of Congress Cataloging in Publication Data

Smookler, Helene V
    Economic integration in new communities.

    (New communities research series)
    Bibliography: p.
    Includes index.
    1. New towns—United States. 2. Discrimination in housing—United States. I. Title.
    HT167.S56   301.36'3'0973   76–18298
    ISBN 0–88410–457–5

Dedication

To My Parents

❋

Contents

✳

List of Figures

List of Tables

Preface

This volume is one of a series of books that summarizes the results of a nationwide study and evaluation of new community development in the United States. The study was initiated in May 1972 under the direction of Dr. Shirley F. Weiss, principal investigator, and co-principal investigators Dr. Raymond J. Burby, III, Dr. Thomas G. Donnelly, Dr. Edward J. Kaiser and Dr. Robert B. Zehner, at the Center for Urban and Regional Studies of The University of North Carolina at Chapel Hill. Financial support for the project was provided by the Research Applied to National Needs Directorate of the National Science Foundation.

The New Communities Study grew out of our concern for the lack of information about the outcomes of new community development in this country. When the original prospectus for the study was prepared, new community development was attracting an increasing amount of attention from both the private and the public sectors. Beginning with a few pioneering new community projects started in the 1940s and 1950s, such as Park Forest and the Levittowns, the 1960s saw a significant expansion in community building. By the end of the decade, over sixty private new community ventures were reported to be under development in eighteen states. The prospect for further expansion in new community development was greatly enhanced by the passage of Title IV of the 1968 Housing and Urban Development Act and the Urban Growth and New Community Development Act of 1970, which provided federal loan guarantees and other forms of assistance for approved new community projects. In the early 1970s, officials of the Department of Housing and Urban

Development were confidently projecting that ten new communities per year would be started under the federal new communities program.

Increasing public involvement in community building was accompanied by heightened expectations about the public benefits that would result from new community development. The Urban Growth and New Community Development Act of 1970 indicated that the Congress expected new communities to improve the quality of life in the nation by: (1) increasing for all persons, particularly members of minority groups, the available choices of locations for living and working; (2) helping to create neighborhoods designed for easier access between the places where people live and the places where they work and find recreation; and (3) providing adequate public, community, and commercial facilities (including facilities needed for education, health and social services, recreation and transportation). Congressional expectations about the benefits from new community development, however, were not shared by all observers of the new communities movement.

On the basis of an in-depth study of new communities in California conducted in the mid-1960s, Edward P. Eichler and Marshall Kaplan (1967, p. 160) concluded that, ". . . community building, even with public aid or under public sponsorship, can do little to solve the serious problems confronting American society." Three years later William Alonso reviewed many of the potential benefits of new community development, but ended up by concluding that, "On the whole, a national policy of settling millions of people in new towns is not likely to succeed and would not significantly advance the national welfare if it could be done" (1970, p. 16). The Twentieth Century Fund Task Force on the Governance of New Towns, which reported its findings in 1971, felt that few large-scale developments in the United States were living up to the promise of the new community concept, and Clapp (1971, p. 287) concluded that existing public programs ". . . to date appear inadequate to further the satisfaction of the major objectives of the new town concept."

Obviously, whether the benefits from new community development are real or imagined is a matter of crucial importance in the formulation of national urban growth policies. Since passage of the 1968 and 1970 federal new communities legislation, seventeen new communities have been approved for assistance. Loan guarantee commitments by the federal government now total $361 million. When completed in about twenty years, these new communities are expected to house almost one million persons, with private investments running into billions of dollars. Given the conflicting opinions about the benefits of new communities and the major public and private investments involved in their development, it seemed appropriate to propose, and for the National Science Foundation to support, a full-scale evaluation of new communities now under development in the United States.

The need for objective information about the performance of new communities has been further underscored by the devastating impacts of the national economic recession, which has produced severe financial problems for the projects participating in the federal new communities program. During 1974 no new loan guarantee commitments were made by the New Communities Administration in the Department of Housing and Urban Development, and on January 14, 1975, the Department suspended further processing of applications for assistance. Faced with mounting financial difficulties with assisted projects, attention within the federal government and the new communities industry has shifted away from the outputs of the program to more pressing concerns for the economic viability of assisted new community ventures. However, the outputs of the program cannot be ignored. If new communities are to receive continued and expanded federal support, they not only must survive as financially viable undertakings, they must also produce benefits that could not be as readily achieved through conventional urban growth.

THE NEW COMMUNITIES STUDY

The University of North Carolina New Communities Study was undertaken to provide federal, state and local officials, as well as public and private developers, with an improved information base to use in judging the merits of new community development as an urban growth alternative. To assure that new communities do, in fact, realize the "quality of life" objectives set forth by the Congress, the study also sought to determine the critical factors affecting the success or failure of new communities in attracting socially balanced populations and meeting the needs of all of their residents.

In pursuing these two goals, the new communities study was designed to provide answers to five major policy questions: (1) Are federally guaranteed new communities contributing more to residents' quality of life than non-guaranteed new communities and less planned environments? (2) Which characteristics of housing, neighborhood design, community facilities and governmental mechanisms contribute most to the quality of life of new community residents, including minorities, low-income families, the elderly, and teenagers?

(3) Which factors in the developer decision process lead to new community characteristics that contribute most to the quality of life of new community residents? (4) How has the federal new community development program influenced developer decisions regarding housing, neighborhood design, community facilities, and governmental mechanisms? (5) How can the federal new community development program be applied most effectively to produce communities which promise to improve the quality of life of their residents?

The research design that was formulated to answer these questions is based on the belief that an evaluation of new community development must involve more than a study of new communities. To provide a sound basis for conclusions about new community performance, comparisons using the same measurement techniques must be made between new communities and alternative conventional forms of urban development. This research strategy led to the selection of a sample of seventeen communities to represent different types of new communities that are under development in the United States and nineteen conventional communities. The new community sample includes two communities that are participating in the federal new communities program, thirteen nonfederally assisted new communities that were initiated prior to the federal program, and two retirement new communities designed specifically for older households. Fifteen of the conventional communities were selected by pairing each of the two federally assisted and thirteen nonfederally assisted new communities with a nearby community containing housing similar to that available in the new community in terms of age, type and price range. Because the paired conventional communities did not have sufficient black and low- and moderate-income populations for comparison with the new communities, four additional conventional communities were selected. These included two suburban communities with subsidized housing and two suburban communities with predominantly black residential areas.

Data collection in the sample new and conventional communities was begun during the spring of 1973 and continued through the summer of 1974. Four types of information were assembled to answer the research questions. First, data on people's attitudes and behavior were collected through 90-minute interviews with 5511 new and conventional community adult residents and self-administered questionnaires returned by 974 young adults (age fourteen to twenty) living in the sample communities. Second, data about community characteristics, including the number, accessibility and quality of facilities and services available and selected housing and neighborhood characteristics, were obtained from community inventories completed for all thirty-six sample communities and from interviews with professional personnel serving the communities. Third, professionals' observations about the communities, as well as factual information about community service systems, were collected through interviews with 577 professional personnel, including school district superintendents, school principals, health officials and practitioners, recreation administrators and community association leaders. Finally, the plans and activities of developers, governments and other institutions involved in the development of the new and conventional communities were secured during preliminary reconnaissance interviews in each community, two waves of interviews with developer personnel, accounts published in newspapers and other secondary sources, discussions with local governmental officials and also from the professional personnel survey.

NEW COMMUNITIES U.S.A.

The major findings and conclusions emerging from the new communities study are summarized in *New Communities U.S.A.* (D.C. Heath & Co., 1976). Capsuling three years of research, the summary report focuses on the strengths and weaknesses of new community development in the United States, key factors which account for variation in new community performance, and public policy options.

In comparison with conventional modes of suburban growth and development, new communities were found to be superior in five major respects. *First*, better land use planning and community design resulted in the provision of a wider choice of housing types for purchase or rent, more neighborhood amenities and services, and safer access to them. *Second*, new community households tended to accumulate less annual automobile mileage, in part because of consistently better access to community facilities and services. *Third*, new communities were characterized by better recreational facilities and services, which resulted in somewhat higher participation in outdoor recreational activities and much higher levels of resident satisfaction with community recreational service systems. *Fourth*, new community residents tended to give higher ratings to the overall livability of their communities and were more likely than conventional community residents to recommend their communities as particularly good places to which to move. *Fifth*, new communities were found to provide more satisfying living environments for target populations— black households, low- and moderate-income residents of subsidized housing, and older persons—than the comparison conventional communities.

Given these benefits and assuming that the costs of new community development are no greater than those incurred in conventional urban growth, the study findings provide ample justification for federal efforts to encourage the increased production of new communities in this country. In fact, federal participation in the new communities field appears to be necessary if new communities are to serve as one means of achieving the goals set forth by the Congress in the Urban Growth and New Community Development Act of 1970.

While producing substantial benefits, new community development in the United States has fallen short of achieving the full potential of the new community concept for solving urban problems and creating a better urban environment. Aspects of community development and life where few overall differences were found between the new and conventional communities studied included: evaluations of housing and neighborhood livability; residents' social perspectives, rates of participation in neighboring, community organizations, and community politics and satisfaction with various life domains and with life as a whole; the provision of some community services; and the organization and operation of community governance. Clearly, in some cases planners have been overly optimistic about the influence of improvements in the physical environment on people's attitudes and behavior. However, in many cases, including the attainment of population balance and the provision of superior public services, the gap between concept and reality can be traced to a variety of factors subject to change through public policy.

In order to optimize the potential that new communities offer for a quantum improvement in the character of urban growth and development, some means must be found to overcome the private developer's limited ability to assume public sector responsibilities and local government's inability to cope with fragmented urban service responsibilities and the debilitating effects of insufficient financial resources. The need to assist developers and local governments in the provision of public and community services was recognized in the Urban Growth and New Community Development Act of 1970, but many of the provisions of the act designed to achieve this purpose were never implemented.

With the federal new communities program at a standstill, two basic, though not mutually exclusive, policy options are available. First, given waning developer interest in larger scale new communities, the program could be reoriented toward smaller scale planned unit developments, villages, and experimental new communities. At the same time that assistance is directed toward smaller scale development, the existing new communities legislation could be amended to recharge those new communities already participating in the federal program. This would require expanded support for low- and moderate-income housing in new communities and the design of new incentives for the provision of high quality and innovative community service systems. Additionally, eligibility for such assistance could be extended to new communities not now federally assisted, if they subscribe to the goals of the program.

Another option, not excluded by the first, would be to return to the basic purposes embraced in the 1970 Urban Growth and New Community Development Act and link the production of new communities to the implementation of a national urban growth policy. If new communities are to be an integral part of a national urban growth policy, stronger measures than exist in current legislation for private developer and state and local government participation in new community development must be provided. This would require full funding and implementation of the 1970 new communities legislation as a first step. Beyond this, federal incentives are needed to encourage state government participation in new community projects, including state oversight of land use and development regulations, state initiatives to establish new governmental structures for new communities, and state financial assistance in meeting the public overhead and front-end costs of new community development projects.

NEW COMMUNITIES RESEARCH SERIES

The seven volumes in the *New Communities Research Series*, published by Ballinger Publishing Company, explore in depth key facets of new community development in the United States. The books in this series are designed to give community development professionals and researchers in architecture, design, education, health care, housing, planning, recreation, social services, transportation and allied professions a fuller and more detailed description and analysis of the new community experience than could be provided in a summary report. In addition to their utility to persons concerned with new community development, these books summarize the results of a pioneering social science research effort. They report the findings of one of the first, and probably the most comprehensive, attempts to trace through sequences of actions and consequences in the community development process—from the decisions which led to the provision of housing and the production of facilities and services through their effects on individual and household attitudes and behavior.

A central premise of the new community concept has been that through comprehensive planning better relationships can be attained among many of the key variables that influence travel behavior. In *Access, Travel and Transportation in New Communities*, Robert B. Zehner examines the availability of transportation and other community facilities and services in new communities and how they influence travel behavior. Particular attention is given to alternatives to the automobile, including walking and community transit, the journey to work, automobile ownership rates and annual household automobile mileage. By analyzing relationships between demographic and community characteristics on the one hand, and residents' travel behavior on the other, Dr. Zehner shows how community design can result in reduced travel and potential energy savings.

Economic Integration in New Communities: An Evaluation of Factors Affecting Policies and Implementation, by Helene V. Smookler, describes the processes of income and racial integration (and nonintegration) in fifteen new communities. The communities are analyzed to determine what factors made integration possible and how they contributed to the effectiveness of the integration programs and strategies that were utilized. The early effects of federal involvement in new community development are described. Dr. Smookler also examines the correlates of residents' integration attitudes, showing that significant differences in attitudes characterize communities with varying amounts of income and racial integration. Finally, the benefits of integration are analyzed in terms of the actual attitudes and perceptions of low-income and black residents living in integrated new communities.

Planned new communities have been viewed as ideal settings in which to develop better ways of organizing and delivering health care services. As described in *Health Care in New Communities*, by Norman H. Loewenthal and Raymond J. Burby, III, however, a number of factors have prevented many new communities from achieving this potential. In addition to describing the approaches to health care that have characterized community building in the United States, the authors examine the impacts of available health care resources on residents' satisfaction with and utilization of health care facilities and services. Health care resources that are analyzed in the study include the provision of physicians' services, hospital care and ambulance service, social service programs, nursing and convalescent care facilities, public health facilities and health maintenance programs. Objective characteristics of health care systems, residents' attitudes and behavior, and health professionals' evaluations are interrelated and used as a basis for the formulation of health care policies for the next generation of new communities to be built in this country.

During the past five years increasing interest has been expressed in the quality of life in the United States and how it can and should be measured. The strategy used to assess the quality of life of new and conventional community residents, reported in *Indicators of the Quality of Life in New Communities,* by Robert B. Zehner, is eclectic, ranging from measures focused on specific functional community service areas to more global concepts, such as residents' overall life satisfaction. A unique aspect of the data presented in this book is the discussion of residents' individual perceptions of the factors that influence the quality of life as they have defined it for themselves. Dr. Zehner also explores residents' satisfactions with a number of life domains—standard of living, use of leisure time, health, family life, marriage and work, among others. He also shows how satisfaction with each domain relates to satisfaction with life as a whole. Differences in the quality of life among nineteen classifications of residents, including blacks, low- and moderate-income persons, and the elderly, are highlighted, as well as observed differences in the quality of life between new and conventional communities.

Recreation in New Communities, by Raymond J. Burby, III, provides a comprehensive description and analysis of this key community service system. A comparative evaluation of the experiences of fifteen new communities in developing recreational service systems is presented. Key agents and their roles in developing community recreational resources are identified. Dr. Burby also discusses the administration of recreational service systems, including their governance, approaches to recreational planning and methods of financing facilities and services. The effectiveness of alternative approaches to organizing the provision of recreational services is evaluated in terms of recreational resources produced and residents' use of and satisfaction with facilities and services. Particular attention is given to how the recreational needs of young adults, elderly persons, women, blacks and subsidized housing residents have been met. Recreational service system characteristics that influenced residents' participation in outdoor recreational activities, satisfaction with the facilities and services used most often and overall evaluations of community recreational resources are identified and used as a basis for suggestions about the best approaches to the design and development of community recreational facilities and services.

Who moves to new communities and why? Why are families considering moving from new communities? What factors attract black families and low- and moderate-income households to new and conventional suburban communities? How do residential mobility processes shape the population profiles of new communities? These and related questions are addressed in *Residential Mobility in New Communities: An Analysis of Recent In-movers and Prospective Outmovers*, by Edward J. Kaiser. In this book, Dr. Kaiser examines the inflow of residents to new communities, paying particular attention to the characteristics of recent in-movers, their reasons for selecting a home in a new community and the improvements that were realized as a result of the move. Because the number and profile of outmovers influence the profile of residents left behind, Dr. Kaiser also examines the rate and type of household being lost to new communities through out-mobility. The characteristics of those households most likely to move are identified, together with the key reasons for their moving intentions. Separate chapters are devoted to the retrospective residential choices and prospective mobility of black households, subsidized housing residents and the residents of federally assisted new communities.

The last book in the series, *Schools in New Communities*, by Raymond J. Burby, III, and Thomas G. Donnelly, examines school development processes and outcomes in the sample of new and conventional communities. Five topics are covered in this study. First, the capacity of school districts to cope with large-scale community development projects is examined through an analysis of the experiences of twenty-seven school districts in developing educational programs for and building new schools in nonfederally and federally assisted new communities. School districts' experiences in serving new communities are traced from each district's initial contacts with developers, through various phases of the school development process, to current issues in the operation of new community schools. Second, school development outcomes are evaluated in terms of both the objective characteristics of school plants and educational programs and the subjective attitudes of educators and parents. Third, links between characteristics of the schools and parents evaluations of the schools attended by their children are identified. Fourth, the impact of school availability on the attractiveness of new communities to various population groups is reported, including the contribution of public schools to households' decisions to move to new communities and their satisfaction with the community as a place to live after they have occupied their homes. Finally, suggestions for increasing the effectiveness of school development processes are offered.

THE RESEARCH TEAM

The New Communities Study, summary report, and monographs in the *New Communities Research Series* were made possible by the combined efforts of a large team of researchers and supporting staff assembled at the Center for Urban and Regional Studies of The University of North Carolina at Chapel Hill. The team members and their roles in the study were the following:

Dr. Shirley F. Weiss, principal investigator and project director, who had primary responsibility for management of the study and coordination of the research efforts of the team of co-principal investigators and research associates. Dr. Weiss's research focused on the overall new community development process, implementation, fiscal concerns and federal assistance, as well as shopping center and other commercial facilities.

Dr. Raymond J. Burby, III, co-principal investigator and deputy project director, who assumed primary responsibility for implementation of the research design and preparation of the project summary report. Dr. Burby's research focused on new community planning and governance, the recreation and leisure service system, schools and health care planning and delivery.

Dr. Thomas G. Donnelly, co-principal investigator, who assumed primary responsibility for the extensive data processing for the study. Dr. Donnelly's research focused on the development and utilization of efficient computation routines for the data analyses and on educational development processes in new communities.

Dr. Edward J. Kaiser, co-principal investigator, who helped formulate the original research design and research management strategy, and offered invaluable advice throughout the study. Dr. Kaiser's research focused on residential mobility processes in new communities.

Dr. Robert B. Zehner, co-principal investigator, who assumed primary responsibility for the design and conduct of the household survey. Dr. Zehner's research focused on transportation and travel in new communities, neighborhood and community satisfaction and the quality of life of new community residents.

David F. Lewis, research associate, who prepared a comparative analysis of the population characteristics of new communities, their host counties and host SMSAs, and contributed to the analysis of housing and neighborhood satisfaction in new communities.

Norman H. Loewenthal, research associate, who undertook a major portion of the professional personnel survey design and field work and assumed primary responsibility for the analysis of health care service systems in new communities.

Mary Ellen McCalla, research associate, who assumed responsibility for immediate supervision of the household survey sampling, field work, and coding operations, supervision of the community inventory map measurement and professional personnel survey coding, and contributed to the analysis of the social life of new communities.

Dr. Helene V. Smookler, research associate, who assumed primary responsibility for the design and conduct of developer decision studies and the analysis of economic integration in new communities.

Invaluable assistance throughout the study was provided by Barbara G. Rodgers, who served as administrative aide, research assistant and publications manager.

The research work was supported by a staff of technical specialists, research assistants, interviewers, coders and office personnel too extensive for a complete listing. In particular, the efforts of the following persons should be recognized: research assistants Jerry L. Doctrow, Mary C. Edeburn, Leo E. Hendricks, Christopher G. Olney and Raymond E. Stanland, Jr.; and, secretaries Cathy A. Albert, Lisa D. McDaniel, Linda B. Johnson, Lucinda D. Peterson and Diana Pettaway.

THE NATIONAL SCIENCE FOUNDATION

The new communities study was made possible by research grant APR 72—03425 from the Research Applied to National Needs Directorate of the National Science Foundation. Throughout the course of the study, the research team benefited greatly from the continuing interest and constant encouragement of Dr. George W. Baker, the project's program manager. Dr. Baker worked with the research team to achieve scientific excellence in each phase of the study.

Of course, the findings, opinions, conclusions or recommendations arising out of this research grant are those of the authors and it should not be implied that they represent the views of the National Science Foundation.

SITE AND ADVISORY COMMITTEES

The process of refining the initial research design was aided by the expert advice of the Site Visit Committee and the panel of anonymous peer reviewers whose ideas were synthesized by Dr. George W. Baker.

An important source of guidance and consultation was made

possible by the project's Advisory Committee, drawn from experts in new community development, city planning, economics, political science and sociology. Jonathan B. Howes, Director, Center for Urban and Regional Studies, The University of North Carolina at Chapel Hill, ably served as chairman of the Advisory Committee which included: Dr. George W. Baker, National Science Foundation; Professor F. Stuart Chapin, Jr., The University of North Carolina at Chapel Hill; Dr. Amos H. Hawley, The University of North Carolina at Chapel Hill; Morton Hoppenfeld, The Rouse Company (resigned March 5, 1975); Dr. Richard M. Langendorf, University of Miami; Floyd B. McKissick, McKissick Enterprises, Inc.; Dr. Frederick A. McLaughlin, Jr., New Communities Administration, Department of Housing and Urban Development (appointed in 1973); Dr. Peter H. Rossi, University of Massachusetts; Dr. Joseph J. Spengler, Duke University; Dr. Lawrence Susskind, Massachusetts Institute of Technology; Dr. Dorothy S. Williams, Department of Housing and Urban Development (1972–73); and Dr. Deil S. Wright, The University of North Carolina at Chapel Hill.

While their collective and individual contributions to the conduct of the study are gratefully acknowledged, it goes without saying that neither the Site Committee, the Advisory Committee nor any individual members bear responsibility for the findings and interpretations in the *New Communities Research Series* and other publications of the project.

NEW COMMUNITIES POLICY APPLICATIONS WORKSHOP

A New Communities Policy Applications Workshop was held in Chapel Hill at The University of North Carolina from November 17 to 19, 1974. The workshop brought together invited representatives of federal, state, local, private and academic user communities to review the methodology and preliminary findings of the study. The workshop was structured to assure that critical feedback to the research team would be secured from formal and informal discussion sessions and to provide a forum for the consideration of broad issues in new community development.

The Policy Applications Workshop was an invaluable part of the research process. The following participants offered many astute observations and critical comments which were helpful to the research team.

Representing the federal government: Dr. Harvey A. Averch, National Science Foundation; Dr. George W. Baker, National Science

Foundation; Bernard P. Bernsten, U.S. Postal Service; Larry W. Co-
law, Tennessee Valley Authority; Dr. James D. Cowhig, National
Science Foundation; Dr. Frederick J. Eggers, U.S. Department of
Housing and Urban Development; Richard L. Fore, U.S. Department
of Housing and Urban Development; James L. Gober, Tennessee Valley Authority; George Gross, House Budget Committee, U.S. House
of Representatives; Charles A. Gueli, U.S. Department of Housing
and Urban Development; Benjamin McKeever, Subcommittee on
Housing of the Committee on Banking and Currency, U.S. House of
Representatives; Dr. Frederick A. McLaughlin, Jr., U.S. Department
of Housing and Urban Development; Paul W. Rasmussen, U.S. Department of Transportation; Dr. Salvatore Rinaldi, U.S. Office of
Education; Ali F. Sevin, Federal Highway Administration; Dr. Fred-
erick T. Sparrow, National Science Foundation; Otto G. Stolz, U.S.
Department of Housing and Urban Development; Jack Underhill,
U.S. Department of Housing and Urban Development; Margaret L.
Wireman, U.S. Department of Housing and Urban Development; and
Theodore W. Wirths, National Science Foundation.

Representing state, local, and community government: D. David
Brandon, New York State Urban Development Corporation; W.C.
Dutton, Jr., The Maryland—National Capital Park and Planning Com-
mission; Brendan K. Geraghty, Newfields New Community Autho-
rity; James L. Hindes, Office of Planning and Budget, State of Geor-
gia; Mayor Gabrielle G. Pryor, City of Irvine, Calif.; Roger S. Ralph,
Columbia Park and Recreation Association; Anne D. Stubbs, The
Council of State Governments; and Gerald W. von Mayer, Office of
Planning and Zoning, Howard County, Md.

Representing new community developers: James E. Bock, Gerald
D. Hines Interests; Dwight Bunce, Harbison Development Corpora-
tion; David J. Burton, Harbison Development Corporation; Gordon
R. Carey, Warren Regional Planning Corporation; David Scott Carl-
son, Riverton Properties, Inc.; Eva Clayton, Soul City Foundation;
Mark H. Freeman, League of New Community Developers; Morton
Hoppenfeld, DEVCO—The Greater Hartford Community Develop-
ment Corporation; Joseph T. Howell, Seton Belt Village; Floyd B.
McKissick, The Soul City Company; Richard A. Reese, The Irvine
Company; Jeffrey B. Samet, Harbison Development Corporation;
Elinor Schwartz, League of New Community Developers; Michael D.
Spear, The Rouse Company; and Francis C. Steinbauer, Gulf-Reston,
Inc.

Representing public interest groups and new community/urban
affairs consultants: Mahlon Apgar, IV, McKinsey and Company;
Evans Clinchy, Educational Planning Associates; Ben H. Cunning-

ham, The Hodne-Stageberg Partners; Harvey B. Gantt, Gantt/Huberman Associates; John E. Gaynus, National Urban League, Inc.; James J. Gildea, Barton-Aschman Associates; Nathaniel M. Griffin, Urban Land Institute; Guy W. Hager, Planning and Management Consultant; William H. Hoffman, National Corporation for Housing Partnerships; Jack Linville, Jr., American Institute of Planners; Hugh Mields, Jr., Academy for Contemporary Problems; William Nicoson, Urban Affairs Consultant; Dr. Carl Norcross, Advisor on New Communities; Robert M. O'Donnell, Harman, O'Donnell and Henninger Associates; Donald E. Priest, Urban Land Institute; Edward M. Risse, Richard P. Browne Associates; George M. Stephens, Jr., Stephens Associates; Eugene R. Streich, System Development Corporation; and Doris Wright, REP Associates.

Representing the academic community: Dr. Allen H. Barton, Columbia University; Professor David L. Bell, North Carolina State University; Professor Richard D. Berry, University of Southern California; Donald W. Bradley, Michigan State University; William A. Brandt, Jr., University of Chicago; David J. Brower, The University of North Carolina at Chapel Hill; Lynne C. Burkhart, University of Massachusetts; Professor F. Stuart Chapin, Jr., The University of North Carolina at Chapel Hill; Dr. Lewis Clopton, The University of North Carolina at Chapel Hill; Dr. Robert H. Erskine, The University of North Carolina at Chapel Hill; Dr. Sylvia F. Fava, Brooklyn College of The City University of New York; Dr. Nelson N. Foote, Hunter College of The City University of New York; Russell C. Ford, The University of North Carolina at Chapel Hill; Dr. Gorman Gilbert, The University of North Carolina at Chapel Hill; Dr. David R. Godschalk, The University of North Carolina at Chapel Hill; Dr. Gideon Golany, The Pennsylvania State University; Professor Philip P. Green, Jr., The University of North Carolina at Chapel Hill; Dr. George C. Hemmens, The University of North Carolina at Chapel Hill; Dean George R. Holcomb, The University of North Carolina at Chapel Hill; Jonathan B. Howes, The University of North Carolina at Chapel Hill; Frederick J. Ickes, The University of North Carolina at Chapel Hill; Dr. Suzanne Keller, Princeton University; Joseph E. Kilpatrick, The University of North Carolina at Chapel Hill; Professor Alan S. Kravitz, Ramapo College of New Jersey; Dr. Richard M. Langendorf, University of Miami; Dean Claude E. McKinney, North Carolina State University; Dr. Robert W. Marans, The University of Michigan; Susan L. Marker, Bryn Mawr College; Dr. Michael J. Minor, University of Chicago; Professor Roger Montgomery, University of California, Berkeley; Daniel W. O'Connell, Harvard University; Dean Kermit C. Parsons, Cornell University; David R. Paulson, The University of North Carolina at

Chapel Hill; Dr. Francine F. Rabinovitz, University of California, Los Angeles; Dr. Peter H. Rossi, University of Massachusetts; Dr. Arthur B. Shostak, Drexel University; Dr. Michael A. Stegman, The University of North Carolina at Chapel Hill; Dr. Robert Sullivan, Jr., Duke University; Dr. Lawrence Susskind, Massachusetts Institute of Technology; Professor Maxine T. Wallace, Howard University; Dr. William A. Wallace, Carnegie-Mellon University; Kenneth Weeden, The University of North Carolina at Chapel Hill; Professor Warren J. Wicker, The University of North Carolina at Chapel Hill; Dr. Deil S. Wright, The University of North Carolina at Chapel Hill; and Dr. Mary Wylie, The University of Wisconsin-Madison.

Representing the press: Barry Casselman, *Appleseeds* and *Many Corners* newspapers; Thomas Lippman, *The Washington Post*; William B. Richards, *The Washington Post*; and Barry Zigas, *Housing and Development Reporter.*

Foreign observers: Åsel Floderus, The National Swedish Institute for Building Research; and Hans Floderus, Building and Town Planning Department, Avesta, Sweden.

To list all the people who contributed to this study is impossible. Among others, these would include 6485 residents who spent time responding to the household survey interview, the 577 professionals who shared their knowledge and opinions about the study communities, and the 173 informed individuals who were interviewed in connection with the developer decision studies.

A final note of thanks is due the new community developers and their staffs who were generous in making available their time and expert knowledge to the research team. In reciprocation, this series is offered as an aid in their continuing efforts to realize better communities and a more livable environment.

Shirley F. Weiss and **Raymond J. Burby, III**

The University of North Carolina
at Chapel Hill
December 10, 1975

✳

Author's Note

A major portion of the data reported here was obtained through interviews with persons in policy making positions in the fifteen new communities studied, and with others who were in a position to influence decisions related to integration. I would like to thank these informants for their willingness to spend time with me, and for their candid responses to often sensitive questions. From them I learned a great deal about the politics, problems, frustrations and benefits of integration and about the new community development process.

Most of the research was completed from 1972 to 1974, while I was a Research Associate at the Center for Urban and Regional Studies of the University of North Carolina at Chapel Hill. All members of the research team at the Center provided assistance and encouragement. Raymond J. Burby, III, especially helped at key points in the analysis and in the production of this volume. Mary Ellen McCalla and Mary C. Edeburn gave needed assistance on survey research techniques and computer use, respectively. Barbara G. Rodgers, Cathy Albert and Diana Pettaway at the Center, Joan Melanson at Wellesley College, and Mollie Copeland deserve special recognition for the onerous task of supervising the production of and typing the several versions of the manuscript. Throughout the project Professor Francine F. Rabinovitz of the University of Southern California provided invaluable criticism and intellectual and emotional support. I am especially indebted to her. Of course, these people are not responsible for the findings, conclusions or recommendations of the study.

Wellesley, Massachusetts
September 1975

Helene V. Smookler

Chapter 1

Summary of Findings

A policy of dispersal or deconcentration of the poor is evaluated in this study not as a strategy for eliminating poverty, but as one method for ameliorating some of the consequences of a socially stratified society. Historically, most national and local public policies have run counter to this, serving to enhance stratification. Now, faced with the reality of a kind of apartheid—concentration of the poor and minorities in the central cities, the middle class and jobs moving to the suburbs—we are beginning to look for solutions. Dispersal can help some of the poor by providing opportunities for better housing, employment and quality education.

New communities have been suggested as a mechanism for determining whether dispersal of the poor in the suburbs is a chimera. The findings of this study indicate that it is a feasible policy, both economically and politically, and that the results are beneficial for low-income families. It would be pedantic to say, however, that with the building of new communities, *mirabile dictu*, economic and class integration followed. Successful implementation of integration policies requires complicated, long-term planning and the support of residents. While no one formula may be appropriate for all suburban areas or even for all new communities, this study evaluates the factors which both facilitate and hinder policy formation and implementation and analyzes the consequences of integration policies for residents and for the housing market.

While the focus of this study is economic and class integration, racial integration strategies are also evaluated. The two policies are difficult to analyze separately; they are intertwined for various reasons. Poor minorities, especially blacks, comprise a significant proportion of urban populations. And it is difficult, if not impossible, to provide housing for the poor in suburban areas without some kind of government subsidy or assistance. These programs require affirmative marketing. Hence, in most parts of the country economic and class integration policies are, perforce, racial integration policies.

METHODS OF THE STUDY

The findings and conclusions of this study are based primarily on two data sources. The factors that influenced the adoption and implementation of economic and class integration policies were systematically determined from detailed histories of fifteen new communities. Seven of the communities—Columbia, Md., Forest Park, Oh., Jonathan, Minn., Lake Havasu City, Ariz., Park Forest, Ill., Park Forest South, Ill., and Reston, Va.—had some economic integration through the provision of subsidized housing. Eight new communities—Elk Grove Village, Ill., Foster City, Calif., Irvine, Calif., Laguna Niguel, Calif., North Palm Beach, Fla., Sharpstown, Tex., Valencia, Calif., and Westlake Village, Calif.—were not economically integrated. A total of 161 interviews were conducted with persons in decision-making positions and with others who could influence decisions or who were in some way involved with integration issues. Data from these interviews were supplemented with comprehensive plans, reports, housing market studies, newspaper articles and census data.

The attitudes of residents toward housing for low- and moderate-income families and measures of the impact of integration on the quality of the life of lower and higher income families were ascertained through household interviews with a sample of residents in each of the communities. In the new communities a total of 3395 interviews were completed, including subsamples of 274 new community subsidized housing residents and 150 new community black residents. Interviews were also conducted with 281 residents of subsidized housing in three conventional communities—Chicago Heights, Ill., Laurel, Md., and Richton Park, Ill.—in order to control for contextual factors and to compare responses of new and conventional community subsidized housing residents.

Before reviewing the findings of the study, several limitations of the research methods should be noted. The results of the study have been derived from cross-sectional data collected in new and conventional communities during 1973. Although the results of earlier studies and subsequent changes were taken into account where data were available, longitudinal analysis and monitoring of new communities over time will be required for a dynamic view of economic and racial integration in new communities.

It should also be stressed that the new and conventional communities studied were by no means completed communities. Some new communities had gone farther in the development process than others—Park Forest and Sharpstown were almost completed—but, on average, the study new communities had achieved only about a fifth of their target populations. Thus, this is a book about developing new communities rather than completed communities. Particular circumstances in individual new and conventional communities will change over time as their populations grow.

The federally assisted new communities studied—Jonathan and Park Forest South—were in the very initial stages of development. The findings for them provide an early empirical picture of the results of the federal new communities program and benchmarks for comparison with later studies of these two and other federally assisted communities. They should not, however, be used to judge the entire federal new communities program.

THE NATURE AND EXTENT
OF INTEGRATION

Among the integrated new communities, the number of subsidized housing units and subsidized housing as a proportion of the total new community housing stock varied from one community to another. Columbia and Reston each had over 500 units of subsidized housing. In contrast, Park Forest South and Lake Havasu City each had fewer than 100 units. Park Forest and Forest Park not only had a substantial number of subsidized units—about 4 percent of the housing stock in each community—they also had some of the lowest priced ownership and rental market rate housing. Jonathan's 151 subsidized housing units comprised 36 percent of the community's housing stock. In addition, only Jonathan came close to matching the demographic mix of its metropolitan area. In contrast to the commonly held belief that it is extremely difficult to achieve integration of both racial and economic groups, most of the communities that were economically integrated also had minorities of all income levels.

The seven new communities with subsidized housing were integrated on a macro- rather than a micro-level; that is, the housing was separate from other housing in the communities, concentrated in one block or neighborhood. However, only three of the seventeen subsidized housing projects in the seven new communities were isolated from the rest of the community. Columbia had the greatest diversity of subsidized housing types and location. Subsidized housing rental costs and purchase prices were controlled by FHA. Cost criteria, perforce, caused the quality of the units to be somewhat below that of the nonsubsidized housing in the communities. Nevertheless, some of the projects were of excellent architectural quality. Most of the residents of subsidized housing lived as close or closer to various community facilities and services as nonsubsidized housing residents.

The higher-income residents (nonsubsidized) of both the integrated and segregated new communities were demographically similar. They held similar positions, had about the same education, and family composition was identical. Thus, the residents of the integrated communities were not unique. The residents of subsidized housing accounted, on the average, for about 9 percent of the population of their host new communities. In contrast with nonsubsidized housing residents, they represented a distinctly lower status group. They held much lower status jobs. With larger families, they earned less than half the annual income, had less education and more of the households had female household heads. In addition, residents of subsidized housing spent more of their income on housing.

THE DECISION TO INTEGRATE

Based on their integration experience, the fifteen new communities were divided into four categories: (1) those that planned for integration and were successful—Columbia, Reston, and Jonathan; (2) those that did not plan for mix, but were integrated—Forest Park, Park Forest, and Lake Havasu City; (3) those that attempted mix, but as of the spring of 1973 had not achieved it—Irvine and Park Forest South; and (4) those that had no integration goals and as a result were homogeneous—Laguna Niguel, Foster City, Westlake Village, North Palm Beach, and Elk Grove Village.

James Rouse, the developer of Columbia, was the first new community developer to begin to operationalize socioeconomic goals and facilitate their attainment. Rouse's objective of socioeconomic integration in Columbia was not a systematically based philosophy, but a community-based rationale tied to the goal of self-sufficiency of the city. As soon as plans for Columbia began to be formalized, Rouse announced that the major strategy to be employed for achieving a balanced community was to set aside a minimum of 10 percent of all dwelling units for low- and middle-income housing. Rouse also instituted several policies and programs which ultimately had a synergistic effect on socioeconomic integration. One of the most important actions was to advertise widely the social goals of the community. This was underlined by the inclusion of blacks in advertising and by staffing the information booth with blacks. A sliding scale for land prices was also established, with up to a 50 percent reduction for builders of housing for low- and moderate-income families.

Rouse, in effect, created a community with a nonexclusionary ethos. Important actions that facilitated the provision of low-cost housing in Columbia included: (1) the recruitment of key personnel who also had a commitment to socioeconomic integration; (2) early solicitation of strategies for implementation of economic integration objectives; (3) early announcement of economic and racial integration goals; (4) inclusion of goals in advertisements of the community; (5) facilitating the construction of low-cost housing by writing down the cost of land; (6) development of alternate strategies for the provision of low-cost housing; and (7) working with organizations and residents of the community to establish the credibility of economic integration policies.

Robert E. Simon, Jr., the original developer of Reston, did not formalize his concern for social structure in Reston, as Rouse did in Columbia. However, many of Simon's actions facilitated the existence of subsidized housing. He set precedents that the subsequent developer, Gulf-Reston, Inc. followed, often at the insistence of the residents. Actual housing need for families with low and moderate incomes was considered in making many of the decisions in Reston, especially by FHA. The factors considered in determining housing need included the income level of the employees of the approximately 100 firms located in the community, the Dulles Airport facility located nearby and the United States Geological Survey headquarters, which relocated to Reston. In support of socioeconomic integration, Gulf wrote down the cost of land to project sponsors and advertised the economic and social mix of the community.

The third new community that planned for integration and was successful, Jonathan, was the first community in the country to receive a loan guarantee under Title IV of the 1968 Housing and Urban Development Act. However, officials of the Jonathan Development Corporation reported that the developer, Henry McKnight, was committed to the goal of socioeconomic integration, even if the community had not received a federal loan guarantee. The Jonathan Development Corporation followed through on McKnight's commitment to economic and class integration. Subsidized housing projects were constructed in the community and their existence was noted in community advertisements. In addition, the development company brought in some moderate-income housing without federal subsidies.

The developers of Park Forest, Forest Park, and Lake Havasu City did not plan for economic integration. However, they also did not conceive of their communities as being exclusionary. Early decisions were made which, in the long run, facilitated the acceptance of low-cost housing. The developers of these communities encouraged the construction of homes to capture the middle range of the housing market and did not advertise their communities solely with an appeal to higher-income consumers. In addition, both Forest Park and Park Forest are racially integrated. All of these factors contributed to the nonexclusionary ethos of these communities.

Park Forest had two subsidized housing projects. Acceptance of the first project was facilitated by the characteristics of the clientele group—elderly persons, some of whom were former residents of the community. The fact that the second project consisted of both subsidized and nonsubsidized units, its excellent planning and construction standards, and the location of the project in the southeast corner of the community kept its construction from becoming a community issue. In Forest Park the developer became involved in the provision of subsidized housing through default, rather than as part of the planning process. The rationale for the decision to convert an original, poorly designed subdivision to FHA Section 235 subsidized ownership units was purely economic and involved no social objectives. Forest Park's city government readily approved building permits for the project. In Lake Havasu City two factors led to the developer's decision to become involved with subsidized housing: (1) the immediate need for low-cost housing for the community's industrial and service workers; and (2) an opportunity to experiment with an innovative building approach. There were few participants in the decisions concerning the construction of FHA Section 235 ownership subsidized housing—the developer, a builder and FHA—and no protests from the community's residents occurred.

The history of the unsuccessful attempts at implementing economic and class integration policies in Park Forest South and Irvine demonstrate the importance of strong developer commitment to a marketable integrated community. Various decisions made in both of these communities served to vitiate economic integration objectives.

Under its project agreement with the federal government, the developer of Park Forest South was to have provided 500 units of housing for low- and moderate-income families by the end of 1973. However, the developer was able to gain approval of a delay in meeting this commitment in order to develop the character of the community first. By the fall of 1973, no subsidized housing existed in Park Forest South (some subsidized units were later provided by converting an unoccupied apartment building to FHA Section 236 rental units). The first attempt to provide such housing was defeated by the village board of trustees, after it became a major community issue. The defeat of Park Forest South's first subsidized housing proposal could be traced, in part, to the developer's failure to keep the community informed about planning and development proposals and to the decision to build the project in a wooded area, a move that would stimulate environmental protests. In addition, HUD failed to communicate and work with the village government to assure that subsidized housing would be built.

There was no specific mention of providing housing for low- and moderate-income families in the Irvine Plan adopted by Orange County in 1964, and no statements concerning balance or openness were included in The Irvine Company's marketing efforts. Nevertheless, the developer made several aborted attempts at providing moderate-income housing in Irvine. FHA rejected the first proposal on the grounds that too many units were concentrated on one site and that noise from an adjacent freeway violated environmental noise standards. Prior to Irvine's incorporation, The Irvine Company developed a proposal for a 400-acre site with homes to be moderately priced. The county planning commission refused to approve the density. After the city incorporated, the project was revived; but after a storm of resident protests, the density was lowered by the city planning commission, and the price of the units was consequently raised beyond the means of moderate-income households.

The communities of Laguna Niguel, Foster City and North Palm Beach all had to deal with the issue of economic and class integration. In each instance, a proposal for low-cost housing came from outside the community and either the developer, a homeowners' association or a local governmental agency was able to thwart the attempt at integration. In Elk Grove Village, the provision of housing for moderate-income families was proposed by a community group, but was delayed by the village board of trustees. In Sharpstown, Valencia and Westlake Village, economic integration never became an issue and no subsidized housing was constructed.

What, then, accounts for economic and class integration in new communities? Some have claimed that community builders are a new breed of developer who have a special sense of mission. In fact, new community developers, like subdivision developers, are driven by the profit motive. Most developers respond to market demand, not housing need. Only the developers of Columbia, Reston and Jonathan anticipated market need as well as demand. In the case of Lake Havasu City, subsidized housing was the response to immediate demand. Forest Park's and Park Forest's decisions were also *ad hoc*. A determination was made that subsidized housing would maximize return on the sites at that time. This was also a factor in Jonathan, which was not located in a "seller's" market.

In many cases, however, market decisions, that created entire cities for the middle and upper classes, raise serious questions concerning the public interest. The issue is raised not only because a large segment of the population is excluded from the new community market, but also because of the impact on surrounding areas.

Developers' marketing strategies had a significant impact on resident acceptance of housing for low-income families. In Columbia and Reston, whose developers pursued open marketing policies, the residents worked to see that subsidized housing was provided. In new communities that were marketed as middle and upper class havens, the residents were often instrumental in helping to defeat proposals for low- and moderate-income housing.

Finally, it should be noted that government intervention occasionally facilitated the provision of subsidized housing in new communities. For example, a result of the federal government's decision to relocate the United States Geological Survey headquarters in Reston was the construction of close to 2000 low-cost housing units in the community. Park Forest's city council played a leading role in securing the community's first subsidized housing project. Local governments serving Columbia, Forest Park and Lake Havasu City generally did not interfere in efforts to build subsidized housing units, and Fairfax County, which serves Reston, took an active role in promoting such housing. However, when a majority of the residents seemed to oppose subsidized housing, local governments, such as those serving Elk Grove Village, Foster City, Irvine, Laguna Niguel and North Palm Beach, were effective in accommodating their wishes.

The major government incentive program for economic and class integration of the suburbs is the federal new communities program. It is difficult to determine the influencing role of involvement with the federal program in Jonathan's and Park Forest South's integration policies. It is safe to assume, however, that there was not a straight causal relationship between participation in the federal program and provision of subsidized housing. Looking at the record of other new communities participating under the 1970 federal new communities legislation does not provide any evidence to support the contention that the federal government is helping to fill a void created by strictly private development. The provision of housing for low- and moderate-income families appears to be concomitant with the generally slow development and financial difficulties of the federally assisted new communities. However, given the inchoate status of the new communities program and the problems in staffing and administrative support, a wholesale indictment of the federal involvement is inappropriate.

RESIDENTS' ATTITUDES
TOWARD INTEGRATION

Among the key factors that affected the feasibility and stability of integration were the levels of residents' tolerance and prejudice. The findings of this study provide some credibility for the assertion that it is becoming easier to integrate racially than by class. However, racial prejudice was also evident. For all respondents in the household survey, opposition to housing for low- and moderate-income families varied according to the race and life cycle of these families. For example, there was less resistance to housing for retired persons earning less than $5000 annually than for other families in that income category. While opposition to blacks decreased as their incomes went up, it was still greater than opposition to whites in all income and life cycle categories.

The key variables that consistently accounted for variance in residents' integration attitudes were: (1) the existence of subsidized housing in a new community; (2) the value of the respondent's dwelling unit; (3) whether the respondent owned or rented; and (4) a contextual variable that measured concern for social status. In the first case, the data indicate that respondents who lived in integrated communities, particularly those who lived in close proximity to subsidized housing, were most likely to support economic integration. Low status concern also correlated highly with positive integration attitudes. The two dwelling-unit characteristics, high value and ownership, related strongly to opposition to economic mix. Individual attributes, such as age, race, income and occupation, while significant on some of the measures did not account for most of the variance in integration attitudes.

EFFECTS OF INTEGRATION ON
LOW-INCOME RESIDENTS

Respondents living in subsidized housing in the new and conventional communities were asked to compare their dwelling unit, neighborhood, community and facilities to their previous place of residence. Except for one measure, the new community residents of subsidized housing consistently evaluated their present residence more favorably. In addition, compared to subsidized housing respondents living in conventional communities, new community residents living in subsidized housing gave much higher evaluations of community components and were more satisfied with the impact of the move to the community on their quality of life. Almost three times as many said that they would advise friends and relatives to move to the new communities.

Concern has been expressed over the possible social isolation of lower-status persons in the potentially hostile environment of a middle class new community. This concern appears to be unwarranted. Low-income residents in the new communities did not appear to be at all isolated. They had more interaction with friends and relatives than their higher income neighbors or than the respondents who were living in the conventional communities. They did not differ in their perceptions of whether people were alike in their communities. Nor did the lower status families see their neighbors as hostile.

EFFECTS OF INTEGRATION ON
THE HOUSING MARKET

The findings of this study indicate that in no case has the existence of subsidized housing adversely effected the housing market or property values in any of the communities. This conclusion is based on interviews with builders, realtors and mortgage bankers in each of the areas where the communities are located, and on comparison of home construction rates and sales with those of surrounding communities.

Securing the investment of property owners in new communities was not a problem. A greater problem appeared to be the ability to control inflated property values. Characteristics of new community development—completed infrastructure and amenities—generally operated against any negative impact on the housing market or property values.

CONCLUSION

New communities appear to be a *de novo* method for integration. The rationale for a policy of economic and class integration in new communities is based partly on the premise that they can provide a mechanism for demonstrating that housing for low- and moderate-income families can be designed, grouped and distributed in such ways as to break down middle class hostility to it and to its occupants, while providing a better quality of life for the low-income families. The findings of this study indicate that many new communities have, in fact, been able to do this without a negative market impact. Not only is economic, class and racial integration politically and economically feasible, it appears to be beneficial for the low-income families.

Chapter 2

Deconcentration of the Poor and Public Policy

INTRODUCTION

In the quarter-century since the Congress established "a decent home and a suitable living environment for every American family" as a national goal, housing conditions have generally improved, but not for every American family. The most critical problem today is not the overall quality of housing units, but the distribution of that housing and its residents. We are, as the *Report of the National Advisory Commission on Civil Disorders* (1968) warned, moving toward two increasingly separate societies. Most of the metropolitan poor and minorities live in the central cities, and middle and upper class whites reside in the suburbs. While not all suburbs are affluent, they are socially homogeneous. The major consequence of this distribution is inequality— in housing, education, employment opportunities and other services.

The central cities are not in a competitive position with the communities that ring them. Public policies at the local and national level have not provided leverage to balance the inequities. In fact, the social stratification has been exacerbated by many governmental programs. Ideally, public policies should be directed toward eliminating poverty. Instead, the policies that have helped produce social stratification are retained and programs are proposed to ameliorate the consequences.[a] Urban renewal, welfare and other programs, while temporarily supporting inner city residents and services, fail to per-

[a]See Frances Fox Piven and Richard A. Cloward (1971) for a critique of our social welfare system and its goals.

manently alter decaying conditions or affect the patterns of residential or racial segregation.

In this chapter the patterns and consequences of residential and racial segregation are described and the rationale for an alternative strategy—dispersal—is presented. Dispersal is not discussed as an illustration of the only strategy for dealing with the inequities of segregation. In fact, dispersal policies without concomitant programs for the central cities could exacerbate the problems.[b] It is evaluated in the context of it being a strategy for helping some of the poor by providing them with housing choice. Chapter 3 includes a discussion of new communities as a mechanism for dispersal, a description of the fifteen sampled communities and the methodology of the study. The extent of integration in each of the communities is described in Chapter 4. Factors in the development process which correlate with successful implementation of policies are analyzed in Chapter 5. Chapter 6 includes an evaluation of residents' attitudes and support for integration. The consequences of dispersal for both low- and high-income residents of communities and the housing market are the focus of Chapter 7. Dispersal policy, the new communities context and suggestions for future policy are explored in the concluding chapter.

PATTERNS OF STRATIFICATION

While the central cities' share of the country's population has not changed over the past two decades, the suburbs' share has grown significantly (see Table 2—1). Suburbanization has been occurring since the turn of the century. It accelerated dramatically after World War II, however, and began to drain the central cities of their white middle class. By 1970 suburbs accounted for 84 percent of metropolitan-area growth (see Table 2—2). Accompanying the middle class movement to the suburbs has been the loss of the residential tax base and new industry in the central cities.

Concentration of the Poor

Not all of the poor live in the central cities (see Table 2—3). Those who do live in suburban areas are concentrated in older decaying communities. Homogeneity of American suburban communities is one of their most salient characteristics.

In 1969 more than 20 percent of all central city families had incomes below $5,000. This was almost double the proportion of such

---

[b]Francine F. Rabinovitz (1975) also makes this point. Bennett Harrison (1974) provides an excellent analysis of dispersal proposals.

Table 2-1. Shares of Total U.S. Population by Geographic Areas, 1900-1970 *(percent)*

Year	All Metropolitan Areas	All Central Cities	All Suburbs	All Non-metropolitan Areas
1900	41.9	26.0	15.9	58.1
1910	45.7	29.5	16.2	54.3
1920	49.7	32.8	16.9	50.3
1930	54.3	35.1	19.2	45.7
1940	55.1	34.5	20.6	44.9
1950	59.0	34.6	24.4	41.0
1960 (212 areas)	63.0	32,3	30.7	37.0
1960 (230 areas)	67.0	33.8	33.2	33.0
1970	69.0	31.4	37.6	31.0

Source: Anthony Downs (1973, p. 199). Downs derived his data from U.S. Census sources.

Table 2-2. Total Metropolitan Area Population Growth Occurring in Central Cities and Suburbs *(percent)*

Decade	Central Cities	Suburbs
1900-10	72.1	27.9
1910-20	71.6	28.4
1920-30	59.3	40.7
1930-40	40.8	59.2
1940-50	40.7	59.3
1950-60	23.8	76.2
1960-70	16.0	84.0

Source: Downs (1973, p. 199).

Table 2-3. Distribution of Family Income by Geographic Areas, 1970 *(percent)*

Geographic Area	Below Poverty	Less than $5,000	More than $15,000
Central Cities	12.9	20.8	18.5
Suburbs	7.1	12.2	26.6
Nonmetropolitan Areas	18.9	27.2	12.2
Total United States	12.6	20.0	19.3

Source: U.S. Bureau of Census (1971a, Table 7).

families in the suburbs. The same pattern holds for the number of people below the poverty level, which in 1970 was $3968 for a non-farm family of four. The central cities had approximately 1.8 times the number of people in this category as the suburbs (see Table 2—3).

The impact of this concentration on city finances and services is severe. More important, however, is the impact on the residents in poor neighborhoods. The quality of housing is generally lower, levels of suburban spending for education greatly exceed those of central cities,[c] and crime rates for all serious crime and most other categories are significantly higher in larger cities. Within cities crime is concentrated at the center, usually in the poorest neighborhoods.[d]

Racial Segregation

Between 1960 and 1970 central cities lost a small percentage of their white population (see Table 2—4). In the same period, black population in the cities increased over 80 percent. In spite of the passage of the Civil Rights Act of 1968, which includes a provision stating that it is "the policy of the United States to provide, within constitutional limitations, fair housing throughout the United States," and generally more favorable white attitudes, decline in sub-

Table 2—4. Population Growth in Geographic Areas by Race, 1960—1970
(percent)

Geographic Area	White	Black
Central Cities	−3.4	81.1
Suburbs	84.6	23.9
Nonmetropolitan Areas	18.8	−5.0

Source: U.S. Bureau of Census (1971b, p. 16).

[c]Inequities in the tax base result in widely different levels of educational expenditures. The costs for educational quality are discussed in Betsy Levin, Thomas Muller and Coranzon Sandoval (1973). According to James S. Coleman (1966), for black students socioeconomic segregation in the classroom is more likely to produce poor school performance than are such factors as the qualifications of teachers, the quality of school facilities or the teacher-student ratio.

[d]See especially, *Report of the National Advisory Commission on Civil Disorders* (1968); and Marvin Wolfgang (1970, pp. 271—311). Wolfgang notes that, "Not only do big cities have more crime, within those cities crime is concentrated at the center. The percentage of stores that were burglarized, or in which persons were robbed, decreased regularly from the center of the city (Chicago) toward the city limits, and the decrease continued steadily for 125 miles except in one area where the rate increased slightly because of the presence of a medium sized city. Similar findings were noted for the metropolitan area of Detroit relative to the offenses of homicide, assault, rape and robbery" (p. 273).

urban racial segregation has been small. Most of the 16.3 percent of the black population living in suburbs (see Table 2—5) is concentrated in predominantly minority neighborhoods.

Concentration of the black population in the central cities has a complicated impact on class and racial segregation problems for the minority families. Median income for blacks is significantly lower than for whites,[e] and blacks pay more for the same quality housing than whites (see Chester Rapkin 1969).

Patterns of Employment Growth and Location

One of the most-cited reasons for a policy of dispersal is that most new industry is locating in the suburbs,[f] and many of the jobs traditionally held by blacks are suburbanizing, while there is only token suburbanization of blacks.[g] While it is true that new industry is not locating in the central cities and that the cities retain less than half of the blue and lower-level white collar jobs, the net loss of jobs for the cities has not been dramatic (see Table 2—6). In fact, in certain sectors, such as government, the absolute number has increased (see Harrison 1974 and Amos H. Hawley and Vincent P. Rock 1973, p. 20). However, it is evident that suburbia presents many more employment opportunities and that residential segregation policies and lack of adequate transportation cause many urban poor and minorities to be excluded from that job market.

Table 2—5. White and Black Population by Geographic Areas, 1970 *(percent)*

Geographic Areas	White	Black
Central Cities	27.5	57.8
Suburbs	40.3	16.3
Nonmetropolitan Areas	32.2	26.0

Source: Anthony Downs (1973, p. 199).

[e]In 1974 black median income for a family of four was $7810; for a white family of four, $13,360.

[f]This argument is critiqued by Bennett Harrison (1974, p. 5): "The critical assumption underlying these calculations is that if blacks had the same spatial distribution of residences as do whites, then black access to local jobs would be equal to that of an equivalent white sample. This is a questionable assumption. In a discriminating economy, the existence of large or even growing numbers of suburban jobs does not guarantee that nonwhites will be able to move into these jobs, even if they live nearby."

[g]This is known as the "mismatch hypothesis."

Table 2–6.   Percentage Changes in Employment in 39 Metropolitan Areas, Cities and Suburbs by Selected Industrial Classification: 1948–1967

Year	Manufacturing		Retail Trade		Wholesale Trade		Selected Services[a]	
	City	Suburb	City	Suburb	City	Suburb	City	Suburb
1948–54	3.1	24.3	4.6	68.7	-4.7	34.2	54.6	86.9
1954–58	-9.3	3.1	3.6	-0.1	3.9	46.4	16.2	40.5
1958–63	-1.0	17.1	-10.2	10.0	-3.0	39.3	3.0	26.5
1963–67	7.3	25.9	2.2	22.5	3.7	29.1	3.0	19.2

Source: Neil N. Gold (1972, p. 454).

[a]"Selected services" includes such occupations as hairdressers, barbers, janitors, cooks, waiters, bartenders, firemen, policemen, guards and elevator operators.

DISPERSAL: THE LOW-INCOME RESIDENT

From the perspective of low-income persons, integration is proposed as a democratic strategy for upgrading their quality of life. Dispersal of low-income families in suburban areas, it is suggested, will offer incentive, status and alternate models for behavior.[h]

While aspects of the egalitarian rationale for "opening up the suburbs"[i] are not questioned, many do not share the sanguine expectations. Because of the lack of examples, the feasibility and desirability of class mix are seen as uncertain and problematic. The obstacles cited include the possibility that the poor may not want to move to the suburbs and live "amidst a hostile majority."[j] There will be cultural conflict, such as differences in child-rearing practices and social isolation because of an inability to find friends and get along with neighbors (Herbert J. Gans 1973, pp. 144–145).

This wariness is speculation, based primarily on experiences with racial integration. In spite of the pessimism, the findings of this study indicate that it is feasible and desirable to integrate "diverse income groups representing divergent life styles."[k]

RESIDENTIAL SEGREGATION AND PUBLIC POLICY

The pattern of racial and economic segregation in our metropolitan areas did not occur by chance. Policies made at all levels of government made it possible. In many instances the impact of policies was coincidental; in many cases it was intentional.

[h]The most comprehensive research done on the effect of living environments on low-income families concluded that better housing condition was related to improved health, but the impact on family relations, while positive, was too small to be significant. See Daniel Wilner, *et al.* (1966).

[i]Anthony Downs (1973) has provided the most detailed rationale and strategy for opening the suburbs to date.

[j]In their study of low- and moderate-income families in the Dayton area, Nina Jaffe Gruen and Claude Gruen (1972, p. 25) found that 51 percent of the respondents preferred a new home in their own neighborhood, 44 percent in the suburbs, and 5 percent were indifferent; whites were more positive about living in the suburbs than were blacks.

[k]Sylvia Fava (1970) shares Gans' concern for the possible problems involved in integration. She cites the findings of two studies: the lack of racial interaction, despite physical propinquity, in the South Shore of Chicago (see Harvey Molotch 1969, pp. 878–893); and, while overall balance in English new towns has been achieved, at the neighborhood level there is segregation by social class and "the hoped-for intermingling of classes . . . remains a dream" (B.J. Herand 1968, p. 57).

Federal Policies

From 1935–1950—a period in which about 15 million new dwellings were constructed—the power of the national government was explicitly used to prevent integrated housing. Federal policies were based upon the premise that economic and social stability could best be achieved through keeping neighborhood populations as homogeneous as possible. . . . *The Underwriting Manual* of the Federal Housing Administration . . . advised appraisers to lower their valuation of properties in mixed neighborhoods 'often to the point of rejection.' FHA actually drove out of business some developers who insisted upon open policies (Eunice Grier and George Grier 1968, p. 128).

The Congress has enacted two statutes which are the government's main attack against racial discrimination in housing: Title VI of the Civil Rights Act of 1964, which bars discrimination "under any program or activity receiving federal financial assistance;" and Title VII of the Civil Rights Act of 1968, which states that it is "the policy of the United States to provide, within constitutional limitation, fair housing throughout the United States." Most federally assisted public housing and urban renewal are covered under Title VI. It provides that recipients, such as FHA-aided builders, local agencies and public housing authorities, may be stopped from receiving the benefits of federal programs. Title VII extended civil rights coverage to nearly 80 percent of the nation's housing units. Unfortunately, it provides for enforcement largely by resort to litigation, after the remedies of a prescribed conciliation process have been exhausted.

Both of these statutes have been underutilized. Although the Department of Justice can initiate legal action, the Department of Housing and Urban Development (HUD) is limited to "conference, conciliation and persuasion."

Class, as well as racial, segregation has been enhanced by federal policy. VA and FHA mortgages are designed to finance new housing which is built primarily in suburban locations. In addition, "subsidies for public services and other benefits were bestowed on the suburbs, enticing the middle class out of the central city" (Leonard S. Rubinovitz 1973).

The federal government, especially HUD, does have tremendous leverage to open communities. However, when it was proposed that HUD utilize water and sewer grants to encourage communities to integrate, President Nixon stated that "forced integration is not in the national interest."[1]

[1]This comment was made at a press conference on December 10, 1970.

Since it seems impossible to regulate the market so that all suburbs take the poor, policy must be designed to provide strong incentives. Federal new communities legislation—Title IV of the 1968 and Title VII of the 1970 Housing and Urban Development Acts—was designed to provide the incentives within the market structure. Since the development of large-scale planned communities requires tremendous front-end expenditures and a long gestation period before there is a positive cash flow, the federal government offered loan guarantees and a seeming cornucopia of grants in return for implementation of certain social objectives. Among these was a provision requiring housing for low- and moderate-income families. It is discouraging to report that the euphoric optimism that greeted the passage of this legislation was not justified. The success of the acts is discussed in more detail in the next chapter.

Some housing for moderate-income families ($5000 to $11,000, depending on family size) was built in suburbs from about 1968 to 1972. However, the subsidy programs under which the homes and apartments were built were abolished in January 1973 by the Nixon administration. These home purchase and rental assistance programs have been replaced by a leased housing plan, under the Housing and Community Development Act of 1974. To alleviate concentration of low- and moderate-income families in the same neighborhoods, HUD will give special processing priorities to those developers who can guarantee that no more than 20 percent of their units will be rented to families assisted by the leasing plan.

Local Policies

The greatest barriers to economic and class integration have been established by local communities themselves. State statutes have given cities virtual autonomy over the use of land within their limits.[m] Because most municipalities depend on the property tax and see housing for low-income families as a burden on their budgets, exclusion is viewed as good economics. Resulting zoning decisions are made under the veil of promoting the health, safety, morals or general welfare of the community. Added to the fear of a rise in property taxes and falling revenues, there is apprehension over the possible decline in the quality of the public schools, resistance to paying for the subsidies that housing for low-income families requires, overt racial prejudice and a desire for homogeneity.

[m]Since the United States Supreme Court upheld zoning as a legitimate use of police power in Euclid v. Ambler Realty (Village of Euclid v. Ambler Realty Co., 272 U.S. 365, 1926), the control of land has been exclusively in the hands of local communities. See Rubinowitz (1974) for an excellent legal analysis of exclusionary practices.

The most salient determinant of this desired homogeneity is, most likely, simple snobbery. In this theoretically classless society, the major mechanisms for signifying status are a person's dwelling unit and community. Social status is thus maintained by distance from housing for low-income families. A study of residents in several homogeneous middle and upper middle class California new towns found that the most important result of planning is "class image." This image is a product of "the physical environment that symbolically identifies or expresses the relative social status of community residents to the rest of society" (Carl Werthman, Jerry S. Mandel and Ted Dienstfrey 1965).[n]

Hence, any proposals for integration are met with open hostility in most suburban communities. This is not just true of high-income communities. In Pennsylvania it was found that,

> ...respondents from both high- and low-social ranking communities thought that keeping undesirables out was a very important goal. Further, more residents from all types of communities thought that undesirables moving in was more likely to get their community very aroused than any other issue, including zoning, increasing taxes, poor public service, metropolitan government, and unequal tax burdens (Oliver P. Williams, Harold Herman, Charles S. Liebman and Thomas R. Dye 1965, p. 220).

There are a plethora of devices that local communities can use to restrict housing: zoning ordinances, which can place restrictions on multifamily units, density, lot-size, minimum square footage, number of rooms, mobile homes, number of stories or landscaping, and impose other architectural standards that increase the cost of building; regulations which regulate block configurations, physical improvements, and dedication of public lands; and slow growth provisions in the guise of environmental concerns or as a response to costly sprawl.

Recently, the courts, state legislatures and regional agencies have begun challenging the exclusionary policies of suburban municipalities.[o] Unfortunately, the impact of these strategies has been minimal

---

[n]This desire for homogeneity is the theme of many analyses of suburban residents. For example, based on his experiences in Levittown, Herbert J. Gans (1967, p. 155) concluded that, "residents must be homogeneous or think themselves so." Robert C. Wood (1958, pp. 103–114) cited the importance of homogeneity for the creation of a sense of "community."

[o]For example, in 1973 a United States District Court ruled that the suburbs around Cleveland, Ohio, had refused, on discriminatory grounds, to build low-income public housing. The court ordered the Cuyahoga Metropolitan Housing Authority to create a plan specifying sites in those suburbs that reflect their need for low-income housing. The communities are expected to accept their con-

and the mechanisms and procedures are often not applicable to other settings. Whatever the motivations, suburban communities remain recalcitrant, and our metropolitan areas become increasingly more stratified.

---

stitutional obligations for dispersal of this housing. Two years previously, the Supreme Court refused to review a federal district court decision prohibiting the city of Lackawanna, a suburb of Buffalo, New York, from using its zoning powers in a racially discriminating way to exclude a moderate-income FHA Section 236 housing project from a white neighborhood.

The New York State Legislature created, in 1968, the Urban Development Corporation which was given the power to bypass local zoning ordinances, building codes or subdivision regulations in order to construct low- or moderate-income housing. The 1969 Massachusetts' "Anti-snob" Zoning Act also bypasses local regulations. If a public housing authority, nonprofit corporation or a limited dividend corporation is denied a building permit, they may appeal to the Housing Appeals Committee of the Massachusetts Department of Community Affairs.

The most widely known plan for dispersal of low- and moderate-income housing is the Miami Valley Regional Plan (Dayton, Ohio). To gain compliance from communities in the five-county area, the leverage of A–95 review procedure, under which requests for federal funds are cleared, is utilized. In 1972 the Metropolitan Council of the Twin Cities Area (Minneapolis-St. Paul) also adopted a housing allocation plan which utilizes A–95 review to "encourage" suburban communities to build subsidized housing. (This plan and Fairfax County, Virginia's are discussed in more detail in Chapter 4).

Chapter 3

New Communities
and Integration

Given the resistance of local communities and builders to providing housing for low- and moderate-income families in the suburbs, the least system-disturbing or threatening way to arrive at some deconcentration is to integrate in places not yet built. Most new communities in this country are being constructed on the fringes of metropolitan areas where there are few existing neighborhoods with entrenched social and political prejudices. In addition, the high quality of amenities offered should make a certain amount of economic and class integration more acceptable to middle- and higher-income residents.[a]

The desirability of social balance is a major part of the conceptualization of new communities. This has developed out of the perception of the new community as a microcosm of a city. The concept is given added credibility because of the many unique advantages new communities enjoy: scale of development, usually 2000 or more acres with a minimum population of 20,000; unity of planning and development, with the site owned or controlled by a unified management; comprehensive planning, with facilities and services provided at an early stage of development; and a degree of self-sufficiency through commercial facilities and industry which provide job opportunities.

[a]In a study of attitudes of suburban residents toward housing for low- and moderate-income persons, Gruen and Gruen found that the two programs which did the most to facilitate the acceptance of these families in the Dayton area were "assurances the property values will be maintained and a guaranteed increase in the level of services . . . without any increase in the property taxes" (Nina Jaffe Gruen and Claude Gruen 1972, p. 72).

LABORATORIES FOR INNOVATION

The unique characteristics of new communities and the resulting potential for innovation have led many to look to new communities as "laboratories for cities." They are seen as vehicles for social as well as technical experimentation (see Twentieth Century Fund Task Force on Governance of New Towns 1971). Former Secretary of the Department of Housing and Urban Development, Robert C. Weaver, has said that because of the possibilities "to experiment with new approaches to housing for low- and moderate-income households . . . they should demonstrate how families and individuals of a wide variety of incomes and ethnic attributes can live together" (1964, p. 280).

The federal government's involvement in the new communities' process is partially justified by this view. If both racial and economic integration can be shown to "work" in the new communities that have a federal loan guarantee, perhaps other privately financed developers will follow suit.

In spite of the unique characteristics of new communities and opportunities for innovation and experimentation, most new community developers have chosen not to pursue policies of economic or racial integration. It was stated above that one of the objectives of federal government involvement was to set an example that privately financed developers might follow. The provision for "an adequate range of housing and a variety of housing types for both sale and rental for people of all incomes, ages, and family composition, including a substantial amount for people of low and moderate income, during each major phase of residential development" (U.S. Department of Housing and Urban Development 1971, p. 14208) was crucial for passage of the original new communities act in 1968.[b]

Developers receiving guarantees under the Urban Growth and New Community Development Act are required to provide housing for low- and moderate-income families; but partially because of the inchoate status of new community development, only vague guidelines on how to achieve these goals have been provided. The policy implementation problem appears to center around the term "substantial." The original interpretation was that the percentage of units designated for low- and moderate-income families should match the

[b]The Urban Growth and New Community Development Act of 1970 (Title VII) differs from Title IV of the 1968 Housing and Urban Development Act in several ways. The ceiling of loan guarantees was doubled and the program was extended to public developers. The 1970 Act also extended the number of grants-in-aid programs for which developers would be eligible.

proportion of these families in the metropolitan area. Recently, the connotation has changed. The New Communities Administration has taken the position "that the primary factor in the formula should represent a goal of providing housing for everyone in the New Community who wants to live there" (U.S. Department of Housing and Urban Development 1974, p. 8).

Within six years of the passage of the original act, only seventeen new community developers had received loan guarantee commitments.[c] In addition, only four of these had subsidized housing units completed or under construction (see Table 3–1).

THE STUDY

It would be pedantic to state that integration in new communities will solve the problems caused by poverty or in any major way alleviate the consequences of poverty. What is hoped is that this study will show that integration is feasible, politically and economically, and that it is beneficial for the low-income families.

Most policy analyses consider the goals, plans or strategies for achieving goals and implementation. However, to evaluate programs or policies, information must be gathered on the effectiveness or impact, that is, the capacity of a program or policy to cause change. In order to determine the impact of a policy of economic and class integration, the effect on the quality of life of the lower-income and higher-income families in the integrated community, as well as the effect on the housing market, must be determined.

This is not a study of any one policy, public or private. For example, two of the communities in the study have loan guarantees under the federal new communities legislation. This involvement is evaluated as one of the major factors which might facilitate integration. Although housing for low- and moderate-income families requires some sort of subsidy, the federal subsidy programs are analyzed only as they contribute to the broader policy goals. The communities are studied to determine what factors contributed to policy outcomes and the effectiveness of the programs and strategies utilized. In sum, it is the purpose of this study to determine:

1. The factors which influence the decisions to provide for (or not to provide for) economic and class integration in new communities.
2. The factors which facilitate or hinder the implementation of economic and class integration policies in new communities.

[c]For an analysis of the political problems and issues surrounding the passage of federal new communities legislation and its implementation, see Francine F. Rabinovitz and Helene V. Smookler (1973); and Helene V. Smookler (1975).

Table 3—1. Housing in Federally Assisted New Communities as of December 21, 1973

Community	Guarantee Commitment Date	Total Units (Subsidized and Nonsubsidized)	Development Plan Target for Low- and Moderate-income Housing 12/31/73
Jonathan	2/70	742	394
St. Charles	6/70	418	212
Park Forest South	6/70	135	500
Maumelle	12/70	0	70
Flower Mound	12/70	0	40
Cedar Riverside	6/71	1299	639
Riverton	12/71	174	60
The Woodlands	4/72	121	325
Gananda	4/72	0	60
Roosevelt Island	a	f	f
Soul City	6/72	f	f

Source: Office of New Communities Administration.

[a] State land development agency project: obligations will not be guaranteed by HUD, but project eligible for other program benefits.

[b] Allocated for end of 1974.

[c] 117 units are FHA Section 23 Leasing.

[d] Based on income levels of occupied rental units.

[e] Primarily homes from derelict subdivision, which became part of community through land acquisition.

[f] Not applicable or data not available.

3. The effect of federal new communities legislation on economic and class integration in new communities.
4. The impact of economic and class integration policies in new communities.
5. How the federal new communities legislation and other policies can be applied more effectively to provide choices of locations for living which contribute more to the quality of life of low- and moderate-income persons.

Because the majority of the communities in this study are being developed by private corporations and the concern is with social goals, the actions of the private sector in determining the policy agenda are examined. The assumption is that the private decisions are as important as, or in some cases more important than, those made in the public sector. An attempt is made in this study to deter-

Table 3—1. continued

Subsidized Units Committed Prior to FY 1974	Subsidized Units Completed or Under Way	Nonsubsidized Housing for Low- and Moderate-income Families	FY 1974 FHA Section 236 Allocation
f	129	402[d]	80 (+188)[b]
216	0	0	300
226	46	208[e]	125
172	0	0	0
0	0	0	0
234[c]	669	0	900
240	23	0	180
0	0	0	121
0	0	0	30
f	1003	f	f
f	f	f	25

mine the role and the capacity of both private enterprise and government to accomplish social goals.

RESEARCH DESIGN

The findings and conclusions of this study are based primarily on two data sources. The factors that influenced the adoption and implementation of economic and class integration policies were systematically determined from detailed histories of fifteen new communities.[d] Seven of the communities had adopted policies of economic integration; eight had not.[e] A total of 161 interviews were conducted with persons in decision-making positions and with others who could influence decisions or who were in some way involved with the issue. These interviews were supplemented with comprehensive plans, reports, housing market studies, newspaper articles and census data.

The attitudes of residents toward housing for low- and moderate-income families and measures of the impact of integration on the

[d]Appendix A contains a description of the procedures that were used in selecting communities for the study.

[e]See Appendix B for a comprehensive listing of subsidized housing in each of the communities.

quality of life of lower- and higher-income families were ascertained through household interviews with a sample of residents in each of the new communities. In those communities with subsidized housing, a subsample of occupants was also selected. Residents of subsidized housing in less planned, conventional environments were also interviewed as controls.

As mentioned above, in order to provide housing for low- or moderate-income families, subsidies are required.[f] The extent of economic and class integration is measured by the amount of subsidized housing in each of the communities and the socioeconomic characteristics of the residents. These are objective measures and do not preclude generalizing the findings to other methods of providing housing for the poor.

THE COMMUNITIES

Seven of the communities had some class or racial integration and eight did not. Although the communities in the sample all met the general criteria for new community status (see Appendix A), a range of characteristics was displayed. They differed in location (see Figure 3-1), pace and stage of development, type and current role of developer, governmental structure, age and size (see Table 3-2). While the demographic characteristics of the residents in each of the communities were not identical, the new communities in the sample can be characterized, at minimum, as middle class. This similarity provides a good base line for comparison of the variation in resident opposition or support of economic integration policies.

Irvine, California

The present-day Irvine Ranch of over 80,000 acres encompasses three Mexican land grants. The ranch, owned by a privately held corporation—The Irvine Company—comprises approximately 130 square miles, or one-fifth of the land area of Orange County. The population of the county doubled from seven to fourteen million between 1960 and 1970. Irvine is strategically located in the path of Southern California population growth, 40 miles south of Los Angeles and 80 miles north of San Diego. From the Pacific Ocean, the Ranch extends 22 miles inland. Irvine had a population of 20,000 at the start of the study and plans for 430,000 by the year 1990.

The planning of the nation's largest new community began when

---

[f]This is true whether the subsidy is to the builder or to the low-income family.

Figure 3–1. New Communities

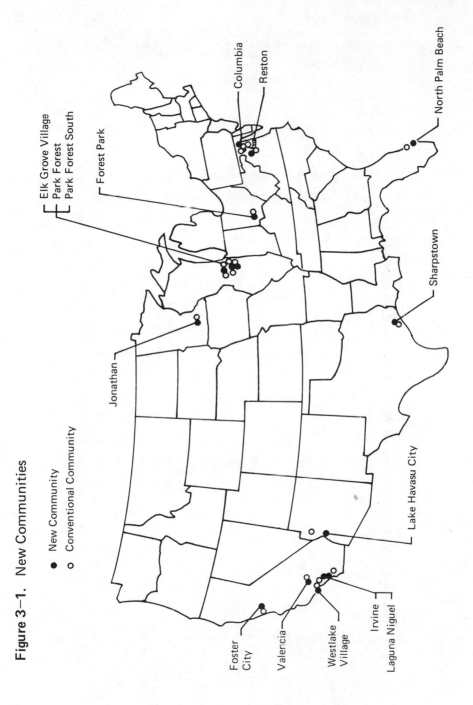

Table 3–2.   Estimated Population and Target Acreage of Sample New Communities

Community	Estimated Population[a]	Percent of Target Population	Target Population	Target Acres
Irvine, Calif.	20,000	6	338,000	64,000[b]
Laguna Niguel, Calif.	8,500	21	40,000	7,936
Westlake Village, Calif.	13,000	26	50,000	11,709
Valencia, Calif.	7,000	28	25,000	4,000
Foster City, Calif.	15,000	42	36,000	2,600
Lake Havasu City, Ariz.	8,500	14	60,000	16,630
Sharpstown, Tex.	34,000	97	35,000	4,100
Jonathan, Minn.	1,500	3	50,000	8,194
Elk Grove Village, Ill.	23,000	39	58,500	5,760
Park Forest South, Ill.	3,200	3	110,000	8,291
Park Forest, Ill.	30,600	87	35,000	3,182
Forest Park, Oh.	17,000	49	35,000	3,725
Columbia, Md.	24,000	22	110,000	18,000
Reston, Va.	20,000	27	75,000	7,400
North Palm Beach, Fla.	12,500	42	30,000	2,362
Total	237,800	22	1,087,500	167,889

[a] At the start of the study in September 1972.
[b] Includes the city of Irvine's incorporated area, sphere of influence and adjacent planning areas.

Irvine was selected as the site for a new campus of the University of California. William L. Pereira had been hired by the University to select a site, with 1000 acres to be donated by the owner. Once the Regents agreed on the Irvine Ranch, Periera was commissioned by The Irvine Company to assist in the planning of the 35,000-acre southern sector of the Ranch. This plan was superseded by the 1970 Irvine General Plan, which took almost five years and more than $1 million to produce. In March 1970 the proposal was submitted to the county for approval.

On December 28, 1971 the City of Irvine incorporated with 18,300 acres. On July 26, 1972 the state local agency formation commission approved a 51,000-acre sphere of influence for the city and the annexation within that sphere of another 8000 acres. Primarily because of the threat of annexation of the large, fast-growing Irvine Industrial Complex by the city of Santa Ana, The Irvine Company supported the move for incorporation.

Demographic characteristics of the residents are presented in Table 3−3. Eighty percent of the residents of Irvine owned their own home, with median home value $42,800. Adult residents had a median of 13.6 years of school and the median yearly income was $19,000. Two percent of the population was black.

Laguna Niguel, California

Also bordering on the Pacific Ocean, Laguna Niguel is located south of Irvine, approximately equidistant from Los Angeles and San Diego. Development of Laguna Niguel began in 1960 under Cabot, Cabot & Forbes. Avco Community Developers Inc., a subsidiary of the Avco Corporation, took over development in 1971. The community is not incorporated and is within the political jurisdiction of the Orange County.

Laguna Niguel's land area of 12 square miles, or 7936 acres, includes a mile and a half of beach front and extends inland 7 miles. The population was estimated at 8500 in 1972, with a target of 40,000 residents by 1983. Home ownership was the highest of any of the new communities (96 percent), with median home value $40,300. Median years of school completed (13.4) and median income ($17,500) were lower than in Irvine. The community was almost exclusively white (see Table 3−3).

Laguna Niguel had a small industrial base. A one-million square-foot, $25 million facility built, but never occupied, by Rockwell International was purchased by the General Services Administration in 1974 to house a branch of the National Archives.

Table 3–3.   Demographic Characteristics of New Community Residents[a]

Community	Percent Black	Percent Homeowners	Median Home Value	Median Years School	Median Income
Irvine, Calif.	2	80	$42,800	13.6	$19,000
Laguna Niguel, Calif.	0	96	40,300	13.4	17,500
Westlake Village, Calif.	2	81	47,500	13.3	21,600
Valencie, Calif.	1	82	37,500	13.1	19,000
Foster City, Calif.[b]	3	71	46,100	13.6	20,200
Lake Havasu, City, Ariz.	0	69	31,800	12.7	12,100
Sharpstown, Tex.	5	88	31,200	13.7	15,900
Jonathan, Minn.[c]	2	62	33,500	13.0	11,800
Forest Park, Oh.	9	68	27,300	12.5	16,400
Elk Grove Village, Ill.	0	83	38,400	12.4	17,600
Park Forest South, Ill.	10	52	30,600	13.1	16,800
Park Forest, Ill.[d]	6	78	24,800	12.9	16,100
Columbia, Md.	19	57	44,100	15.7	17,300
Reston, Va.	4	52	58,000	15.8	19,900
North Palm Beach, Fla.	1	88	35,500	12.8	16,900

[a]Based on household survey of heads of household and spouses, spring 1972.
[b]Approximately 5 percent of the residents of Foster City were Asians.
[c]Jonathan had a total nonwhite population of 3.5 percent.
[d]Park Forest had 2.4 percent other nonwhites.

Westlake Village, California

Located 40 miles northwest of the Los Angeles Civic Center at the south end of the Conejo Valley, Westlake Village is split between Los Angeles and Ventura counties. The Ventura County portion lies within the city of Thousand Oaks. The Los Angeles County portion is not incorporated. In 1964 the land was purchased for $32 million by Daniel K. Ludwig's American-Hawaiian Steamship Company. The 11,709-acre development site is situated in a high growth area which has tripled in population since 1970. Construction began on the first homes in Westlake Village in 1966, and the community had grown to 13,000 residents by 1972. The developers hope to reach a target population of 50,000 (see Table 3—2).

In 1969 The Prudential Insurance Company of America expanded its lender position to that of a general partner with American-Hawaiian. This partnership dissolved in 1972. Prudential retained most of the vacant land and American-Hawaiian concentrated on the management of the income property already built.

The median income of residents of Westlake was the highest of any of the communities in the sample ($21,600). Over 80 percent of the residents owned their own home; median home value was $47,500. The median number of years of school completed and racial composition were similar to those of residents of Laguna Niguel and Irvine (see Table 3—3).

Valencia, California

The land on which Valencia is located was purchased by Henry Mayo Newhall in 1875. He added orchards and field crops to land that was already being used for cattle grazing. The Newhall Land and Farming Company was established in 1883 to administer the land holdings.

Valencia is 32 miles from downtown Los Angeles, 7 miles north of the San Fernando Valley. The area is surrounded by mountains and is located on the major California north-south highway. It has been one of the fastest growing regions of Southern California.

After two years of study, the general plan for Valencia was adopted by the Los Angeles Regional Planning Commission in October 1965. The first phase covered a 4000-acre section at the eastern end of the 44,000-acre Newhall Ranch (see Table 3—2). Initial estimates projected a population of 25,000 by 1975 and a city of 173,000 by 1985. The early population estimates were based in part on the expectation that the Palmdale International Airport would be built nearby in the Antelope Valley. The plans for the airport—to be the largest in the United States—have been suspended, pending environmental and other legal considerations. In addition, a 1971 earthquake was centered in this area, and the widespread publicity of fallen freeway overpasses and bridges hurt sales. Because of these factors and general aerospace layoffs in the area, Valencia's population was estimated to be about 7000 in 1972 and projections at that time were less optimistic.

The characteristics of the residents resembled those of Irvine, with the exception of home values. The median home value was approximately $5000 less (see Table 3–3).

Foster City, California

In 1969 T. Jack Foster acquired 2600 acres of low-lying land, known as Brewer's Island, along the west shore of San Francisco Bay. Brewer's Island took its name from dairy rancher Frank Brewer who drained a major section of the land in 1901. Later, Leslie Salt Company used part of the land for evaporating ponds. In the late 1950s Foster and Richard D. Grant, also a highly successful Bay-area developer, took an option on the land for $200,000. The total land cost was $13 million. Foster subsequently bought out Grant.

In order to finance the reclamation projects required and municipal services, the developer retained a bond counsel to draft legislation that would create the first municipal improvement district in California. The act allowed the district to issue bonds and exempted it from all taxation within the state. The Estero Municipal Improvement District was organized on September 8, 1960. The San Mateo County Board of Supervisors appointed members to the district board of directors. The three men originally selected were Foster's choice. On June 18, 1961 the county board of supervisors approved the general plan and ground was broken on August 25, 1961. By 1969 the bonded debt totaled some $64 million.

Partly because of the high tax rate required to support this indebtedness, a petition drive for incorporation began in the second week of November 1970. The incorporation issue was put to the electorate in April 1971. The vote for incorporation was 2317; against 38. The citizens also voted to make the Estero Municipal Improvement District a subsidiary of the new city government and to make the city council double as the district's board of directors.

Five days before the circulation of incorporation petitions was approved, 1500 acres of Foster City were sold to Centex West Inc., a wholly-owned subsidiary of the Centex Corporation of Dallas, for approximately $15 million.

The first family moved into Foster City in March 1964. By 1972 the population was about 15,000, with a target of 36,000 in 1985 (see Table 3−2). The developers had taken advantage of their bayside location, south of the city of San Francisco, by providing recreational lakes and marina lots. The location of San Francisco Airport just north of Foster City was expected to stimulate growth of the industrial park.

Home values, years of schooling and income of residents were similar to those of Westlake Village. Fewer residents owned their own homes and there were more minorities. About 5 percent of the residents were Asian and 3 percent were black (see Table 3−3).

Lake Havasu City, Arizona

While conducting a flying search for a marine motor testing center, Robert P. McCulloch found Lake Havasu during the late 1950s. The 45-mile long lake, formed by the Parker Dam on the Colorado River, is 150 miles northwest of Phoenix and 235 miles east of Los Angeles. It is a beautiful site surrounded by the Chemehuevi and Mohave mountains.

McCulloch first bought 3500 acres of a peninsula that stuck out into Lake Havasu. In August 1963 he purchased 12,990 more acres of desert next to the peninsula. Later he traded his original purchase for land adjacent to the bigger tract. Because of the lake, climate and beaches, the site had previously served as an Army Air Force rest and rehabilitation center. The land was purchased for about $73 an acre from the State of Arizona.

The city was founded with the intention of establishing facilities for all future McCulloch Corporation industrial expansion. C.V. Wood, a former general manager of Disneyland, completed the master plan in 1963. Lake Havasu City is one of the few freestanding new communities currently under development in the United States.[g] It is planned for a population of 60,000; the 1972 population estimate was 8500 (see Table 3−2).

Lake Havasu City contributed significantly to the 223 percent growth of Mohave County's population during the 1960s. The only larger population area in the county was the city of Kingman. In order to stimulate growth and tourist interest, McCulloch purchased the London Bridge in 1968 and moved it to Lake Havasu City.

More than two-thirds of the residents of Lake Havasu City owned their homes; the median value of the units was $31,800 (see Table 3−3). Compared to residents in the other communities, those in

[g]Another is Soul City, N.C., a federally guaranteed community being developed by Floyd McKissick, former director of CORE. For an evaluation of Soul City's prospects, see Francine F. Rabinovitz and Helene V. Smookler (1975).

Lake Havasu City had completed fewer years of school (12.7) and had the second lowest median annual income ($12,100).

Sharpstown, Texas

Frank W. Sharp began building homes in the Houston area during World War II, developing at one time the largest subdivision in the area—2000 acres. In 1953 he acquired 4100 acres southwest of Houston. At that time the area was far outside the city limits, with no major roads to the site. However, by giving $500,000 worth of right-of-way land, Sharp changed the course of Houston's Southwest Freeway, which now bisects the community. He donated the land with the provision that construction start within one year. Sharpstown is now within the city limits of Houston and the southwest area is one of the fastest growing sections of the Houston-Galveston metropolitan region.

At the time of the study field work, Sharp was only semiactive in development of the community. Most of the home construction was completed between 1954 and 1969. Estimates put the 1972 population at 34,000. While the educational level of residents was similar to the California new communities, the median home value ($31,200) and income ($15,900) were lower.

Jonathan, Minnesota

Jonathan is one of the two federally guaranteed new communities in the sample. In February 1970 the Jonathan Development Corporation received a commitment, under Title IV of the 1968 Housing and Urban Development Act, for $21 million in the form of federal loan guarantees. The community, begun by the late State Senator Henry T. McKnight, is located approximately 25 miles southwest of downtown Minneapolis. Because Minnesota law restrains the creation of new municipalities, Jonathan might have remained unincorporated. However, its developers decided that there were advantages to being annexed to the city of Chaska. In 1967 a new city plan was adopted by Chaska and the creation of Jonathan was publicly announced at that time.

Jonathan Development Corporation expected the community's 8196 acres to have 50,000 residents by 1990. In 1972 the population was 1500. Primarily because of the distance from the central city and competition from closer in, large planned unit developments, growth was very slow during the first half of the 1970s.

Under its project agreement with the federal government, Jonathan was required to provide housing for low- and moderate-income families. At the time of this study, approximately one-third of the dwelling units in the community were subsidized under FHA Sections 235 and 236.[h] This partially explains the relatively low median home value ($33,500) and income level ($11,800). However, median years of school completed by residents (13.0) was comparable to the other new communities.

Elk Grove Village, Illinois

Located immediately northwest of O'Hare International Airport and 26 miles from the Loop, Elk Grove Village has been one of the faster growing suburban communities in the Chicago region. Its industrial park, one of the largest in the country, employed over 27,000 persons in 1972. However, very few of the people who worked there could afford to live in Elk Grove Village.

Centex Construction Company began planning the 5760-acre community in 1956. With a population of 116, Elk Grove Village incorporated in that year. In 1960 the population was 6608; in 1972 it was 23,000. By 1980 the population total is expected to be 58,500 (see Table 3–2).

Elk Grove was neither racially nor economically integrated. Median home value was $38,400; yearly median income was $17,600. The median resident had completed comparably fewer years of school (12.4) than most residents in the other new communities (see Table 3–3).

Park Forest South, Illinois

Nathan and Lewis Manilow acquired the first parcels of land for Park Forest South in 1966.[i] The Village of Park Forest South incorporated the next year. By 1970 the Manilows had added two partners—Mid-America Improvement Corporation, owned by Illinois Central Industries, and United States Gypsum Urban Development Corporation, owned by the United States Gypsum Company.

Park Forest South's 8291 acres are located in Will County, just south of the Cook County line. The community is about 50 minutes driving time from the Chicago Loop. In 1972 the population was approximately 3200, with an expected population of 110,000 by 1985 (see Table 3–2). This target appears to be unrealistic given the slow growth experienced during the first half of the 1970s.

Approximately half of Park Forest South's residents were home-

[h]Section 235 is a home ownership program and Section 236 is a rental program for moderate-income families. These programs are discussed in more detail in Chapter 4.

[i]Lewis Manilow is the son of the late Nathan Manilow who was one of the developers of Park Forest.

owners. Median home value was $30,600. Residents had completed a median of 13.1 years of school, with a median annual income of $16,800. The community was racially integrated; 10 percent of the residents were black (see Table 3—3).

Park Forest South is the second federally guaranteed new community in the sample, receiving a commitment for a $30 million loan guarantee in June 1970. Like Jonathan, Park Forest South is required under the provisions of the federal new communities legislation to provide housing for low- and moderate-income families. At the time of this study, no subsidized housing had been built. Forty-six units of a previously unoccupied apartment building were in the process of being converted to subsidized housing under FHA Section 236.

Park Forest, Illinois

Park Forest is located in Cook County, just north of Park Forest South. One of the first planned communities in the country, Park Forest's development began in 1947 and later received much publicity as the home of William H. Whyte's (1956) "organization man." The developer, American Community Builders Inc., constructed a number of low-cost apartments and houses to provide consumers for a large shopping center planned for the center of the community. The 3182-acre community incorporated in 1949. By 1960 the population had reached almost 30,000, just short of current numbers (see Table 3—2). With the exception of a public housing project for the elderly and a large, partially subsidized planned unit development, there has been little new construction over the past few years and the developer is no longer active.

While Park Forest was not always an open community, by 1973 it was racially integrated, with about 6 percent of its population black and 2 percent "other nonwhite." Park Forest's and Park Forest South's integration stands in sharp contrast to other suburban communities in the Chicago metropolitan area. In 1970 there were only 1000 black families living in white neighborhoods, and 200 of those families were residents of Park Forest. Because most of the homes were comparably older, median home value ($24,800) was lower than in many of the other new communities. More than three-fourths of the residents were homeowners. Median years of school completed and yearly income were similar to those of the residents of Park Forest South (see Table 3—3).

Forest Park, Ohio

Forest Park is located in Hamilton County, 15 miles north of the city of Cincinnati. The land on which Forest Park is located was once part of a 6000-acre parcel assembled by the federal government in the early 1930s for the Greenbelt Program.[j] Six hundred acres were developed and became the city of Greenhills. A flood control project created a 160-acre lake and eventually 2000 acres were turned into a county park.

In the early 1950s the government decided to sell off the remaining 3725 acres. Several concerned leaders in Hamilton County created the Cincinnati Community Development Corporation to make certain that the land would not become "just another housing project." In 1954 the Community Development Corporation sold the tract to the Warner-Kanter Corporation, but retained the right to approve development plans for a period of five years. Victor Gruen Associates prepared the original plan for the community.

The first families moved in during the spring of 1956. The city incorporated in 1961 and adopted the council-manager form of government in 1969. Joseph H. Kanter purchased Marvin Warner's interest in Forest Park in 1959 and by 1973 was only semi-active in current development.

Unlike most other suburban communities in the area, Forest Park was both racially and economically integrated, with 9 percent of the population black and a subdivision of FHA Section 235 homes. Residents of Forest Park had a yearly median income of $16,400, and the median home value was $27,300. Approximately two-thirds of the residents owned their own homes. The community had reached almost half of its projected population of 35,000 (see Table 3–2).

Columbia, Maryland

In 1963 James Rouse, founder of one of the nation's largest mortgage banking firms, announced the purchase of 14,000 acres situated in the Washington-Baltimore corridor. Rouse began acquiring land in 1962, paying an average of $1450 per acre. Connecticut General Life Insurance Company agreed to a loan of $23.5 million and became a partner in 1963.

Rouse hired a large planning staff, including social scientists. During the summer and fall of 1963, work groups, made up of sociologists, economists, psychologists, planners, city managers and others, assisted in the overall design and planning of the community. The initial planning was completed by 1965 and construction began in 1966.

Columbia's 1972 population of 24,000 made up almost 30 percent of Howard County's total population. The community is planned for

[j]For the history of the Greenbelt Program and descriptions of the communities, see Albert Mayer (1967).

an ultimate population of 110,100 on 18,000 acres (see Table 3−2). Columbia was the most heterogeneous community in the sample; 19 percent of the population was black and several subsidized housing complexes had been built. The median education level was 15.7 years and yearly median income was $17,300. Home value ($44,100) was fourth highest of the communities in the sample (see Table 3−3). The most local governmental unit was Howard County. However, Columbia had a very strong and active community association.

Reston, Virginia

Reston was the first large-scale, modern new community in the United States. It is internationally known for its innovation in design. In March 1961 Robert E. Simon, Jr. purchased 6750 acres (eventually 7400) in western Fairfax County, approximately 18 miles northwest of Washington, D.C., for $13.15 million. Simon initially made no arrangements to secure additional funds for future land payments or utilities. When it became apparent that he had underestimated infrastructure costs, he secured a loan of $15 million from the Gulf Oil Corporation.

Fairfax County approved the plans when it established a Residential Planned Community (RPC) zone in 1962 and construction began in the spring of 1963. The industrial park had its first tenants in the fall of 1964 and the first residents moved into Reston in December of that year. Lake Anne Village Center was officially dedicated on May 21, 1966, with notable government officials and planning experts in attendance.

By the end of 1966, Reston's population was only 2500, far short of expectations. Simon had exhausted his financial resources and Gulf-Reston Inc., a subsidiary of Gulf Oil, took over full financial and operational responsibility on September 28, 1967. In 1972 the population was 20,000. It was expected that thenpopulation would reach 75,000 (see Table 3−2).

Like Columbia, Reston was both economically and racially integrated, with several subsidized housing projects and 4 percent of its population comprised of blacks. Median home value was very high ($58,000), as was the median educational level of the residents (15.8 years of school completed). Median yearly income was almost $20,000 (see Table 3−3).

Reston also had an active homeowners association and the citizens had created the Reston Community Association. Fairfax County was the most local governmental unit.

North Palm Beach, Florida

North Palm Beach is a 2362-acre waterfront community located along the intercoastal waterway, 7½ miles north of West Palm Beach. The land was formerly part of the estate of Sir Harry Oakes. It passed successively through the hands of industrialist Ralph Stolkin and then to John D. MacArthur, the insurance magnate. North Palm Beach Properties, owned by Herbert A. and Richard E. Ross, John A. Schwenke and Jay H. White, bought the site for $2,870,000 in 1955. Early land development operations included the dredging of a series of canals and bulkheading all waterfront properties. Almost half of the homesites of this primarily residential community were on a waterway. The developers sold their last parcels in 1967 and by 1973 were no longer active in development. The city incorporated in 1956, soon after development began.

The area in which the city is located has, in recent years, been the best housing market in the country, and North Palm Beach has the highest growth rate in the county. In 1972 the population was 12,500, 42 percent of the target population (see Table 3–2). The community is almost exclusively white. The median resident had completed 12.8 years of school and earned $16,900 annually. The median home value was $35,500 (see Table 3–3).

THE KEY PARTICIPANTS

Selection of Interview Subjects

It was decided that all those who had a formal role in decisions that influenced housing policies in each of the communities would be interviewed: the developer; appropriate local governmental officials (mayors, city council members, city, county and regional planning officials, and housing commissioners); FHA officials; and, for two communities, HUD New Communities Administration officials. The names of persons in each category were obtained during initial visits to each community.

Lists were also made of others who could influence these formal decision makers: consultants; community association officers; fair housing organizations; realtors; mortgage bankers; builders of market-rate and subsidized housing; sponsors of subsidized housing, and other *ad hoc* groups.

In the course of the interviews with the above mentioned participants, names of others who had been involved with economic integration policies in each of the communities were solicited. This process yielded interviews with 161 key participants in the fifteen new communities:

Developers and their representatives	23
Sponsors of subsidized housing	10
Builders of subsidized housing	9
Builders of nonsubsidized housing	7
Local government officials	37
Federal Housing Administration (FHA) officials	11
Mortgage bankers	12
Realtors	12
Fair housing organization officials	15
Managers of subsidized housing	11
HUD new community liaison officer	1
Black leaders (other than above categories)	3
Housing market analysts	2
Other	8
Total	161

The Instruments

After consultation with several developers, FHA officials, builders of subsidized housing and other integration and housing experts, thirteen separate interview schedules were developed—one for each category of respondent and one universal attitude questionnaire.[k] The instruments for each category of participants were designed to determine the history of economic integration policies in the community, the participant's role in the policy making and implementation, the factors that influenced the policy decisions (or non-decisions), and implementation of the decisions at each stage of community development. The attitude questionnaire solicited the respondent's perception of the need for low- and moderate-income housing in the community, attitudes toward racial and economic integration, perception of residents' attitudes, evaluation of the impact of racial and economic integration policies, and strategies for racial and economic integration of communities. All of the instruments were pretested for content validity and timing. Several minor revisions resulted from the pretests.

Initial visits to the communities were made during the fall of 1972. The pretest version of the instruments was completed in February 1973. Pretesting was undertaken in that month and the interviewing took place in the fifteen new communities from March through August 1973.

[k]See Appendix C for a sample of the instruments.

THE HOUSEHOLD SURVEY

In each of the new communities and subsidized housing conventional communities, data on residents' characteristics, attitudes toward racial and economic integration, and use and evaluation of facilities and services were collected as part of 90-minute household interviews conducted in 1973. In the new communities a total of 3395 interviews were completed, including subsamples of 274 new community subsidized housing residents and 150 new community black residents. A total of 281 residents in the subsidized housing conventional communities were also interviewed.[1]

OTHER DATA SOURCES

The above data were supplemented by measurements of distances from the respondents' dwelling units to the nearest facilities and services evaluated in the household survey. In addition to data collected in the field, several secondary sources were utilized: comprehensive plans; city, county and regional housing elements; census data; and housing market analyses.

[1]Sampling and interviewing procedures used in the household survey are summarized in Appendix A. See Appendix D for questions that were used for the analyses reported in this book.

Chapter 4

Nature and Extent
of Integration

Although the communities in this study had a broad range of housing, and resident support for and satisfaction with the housing mix and its impact on the market are analyzed, no attempt is made to determine what constitutes a proper mix. Most social planners seem to advocate a mix that matches the demographic composition of the metropolitan area.[a] That is a difficult, if not impossible, standard to meet. Especially since suburban communities, like those in this sample, are in different stages of development (see Table 3—2) and have disparate employment bases, transportation and service facilities.

It has also been suggested that communities be guided by less portentous goals, such as, "... [that] every community must employ some low-income people and that they should be able to live in the community in which they work" (Gans 1973, p. 146). This implies a strategy for class integration as well as number of residents. In this chapter the nature and extent of integration is discussed. The development process, which either provided for or excluded low-income families, is reviewed in the next chapter.

Because suburban housing for low- and moderate-income families is impossible to provide without some sort of subsidy, the proportion

[a]In its early guidelines for Title VII developers, HUD included as "documentation necessary to determine the required (population) mix ... current regional profile by income, family size and age and the projected profiles for major development periods in the plan ... ; current supply of and demand for standard housing and projections of demand by age, family size and income for low and moderate residents and the elderly for the region and market area ..." (U.S. Department of Housing and Urban Development, 1972).

of subsidized housing and the demographic characteristics of residents are the measures of integration utilized in this study. As mentioned earlier, although racial integration is not the major focus of the study, it is discussed in some depth in this and the following two chapters.

EXTENT OF INTEGRATION

As the data in Table 4—1 indicate, seven of the communities—Columbia, Reston, Jonathan, Forest Park, Park Forest, Park Forest South and Lake Havasu City—had some economic integration through the provision of subsidized housing units. Most of the communities had some nonwhite residents.

Although racial integration existed and the proportion of housing for low-income families was significant for many of the communities, only Jonathan came close to the demographic mix of its metropolitan area (see Table 4—2),[b] However, it should be noted that despite the admonition that, "The most difficult kind of residential balance to achieve is integration of *both* racial and economic groups" (Fava 1970, p. 14), most of the communities that were economically integrated also had minorities of all income levels.

Approximately 7 percent of Columbia's housing was subsidized and 20 percent of its population was nonwhite (19 percent of the higher income population and 39 percent of those living in subsidized housing). Reston provided more housing for low- and moderate-income families, but had fewer blacks. While Jonathan had the greatest proportion of subsidized housing, it had the fewest minorities. Like Columbia and Reston, Forest Park's black population included higher income families as well as those living in subsidized housing. Lake Havasu City was the only community that provided some housing for low-income families but was not racially integrated. While there were very few blacks living in the surrounding area, there was a significant native American population.

TYPE AND SPATIAL LOCATION OF
SUBSIDIZED HOUSING UNITS

The seven communities with subsidized housing were integrated on a macro- rather than a micro-level; that is, the housing was separate from other housing in the communities, concentrated either in one

---

[b]The data presented in Table 4—2 are not meant to imply that persons living in subsidized units had incomes comparable to those living below the poverty level.

Table 4–1. Racial and Economic Integration

New Community	Percent Nonwhite			Subsidized Housing	
	Total	Nonsubsidized Housing	Subsidized Housing	Number of Dwelling Units	Percent of Dwelling Units in Community
Columbia	20	19	39	532	7
Reston	5	4	15	926	11
Jonathan	4	3	4	151	36
Forest Park	9	8	25	201	4
Park Forest	9	9	10[a]	354	4
Park Forest South	10	10	[b]	46	3
Lake Havasu City	<1	0	0	64	3
Sharpstown	5	5	[c]	0	0
Foster City	7	7	[c]	0	0
Irvine	5	5	[c]	0	0
Valencia	3	3	[c]	0	0
Elk Grove Village	1	1	[c]	0	0
Westlake Village	3	3	[c]	0	0
Laguna Niguel	1	1	[c]	0	0
North Palm Beach	1	1	[c]	0	0

[a]Based partially on prerent-up applications.
[b]Units not occupied at time of sampling.
[c]Not applicable.

Table 4–2. Comparison of Socioeconomic Mix of Metropolitan Areas[a] and New Communities (percent)

Metropolitan Area[b,c]			New Communities		
Metropolitan Area	Families Below Poverty Level	Black	New Community	Subsidized Housing Units	Nonwhite
Baltimore	9	31	Columbia	7	20
Washington, D.C.	6	33	Reston	11	5
Minneapolis/St. Paul	5	2	Jonathan	36	4
Cincinnati/Ky./Ind.	8	12	Forest Park	4	9
Chicago	7	22	Park Forest	4	9
Chicago	7	22	Park Forest South	3	10
[d]			Lake Havasu City	3	<1
Houston	10	24	Sharpstown	0	5[e]
San Francisco/Oakland	4	13	Foster City	0	7[f]
Anaheim/Santa Ana/Garden Grove	5	1	Irvine	0	5[g]
Los Angeles/Long Beach	8	13	Valencia	0	3
Chicago	7	22[h]	Elk Grove Village	0	1
Los Angeles	8	13[h]	Westlake Village	0	3
Anaheim/Santa Ana/Garden Grove	5	1	Laguna Niguel	0	1
West Palm Beach	10	21	North Palm Beach	0	1

[a] Standard Metropolitan Statistical Area.

[b] U.S. Bureau of Census 1972.

[c] 1972 figures.

[d] Not in metropolitan area, data not available.

[e] Chicano and black population.

[f] Asian and black population.

[g] Chicano and black population.

[h] Westlake Village borders on the Oxnard/Simi/Ventura Metropolitan Area which is only 1.78 percent black.

block or neighborhood. "Locationally, micro-integration must be pervasive; class or racial integration must exist on every block" (Gans 1973, p. 152). Only Columbia came close to this definition (see Table 4—3).

Columbia had the greatest diversity of subsidized housing types and location. Columbia experimented by locating its first subsidized housing project on five sites in two villages. Although this strategy appears to have been successful, except for a few single-family homes it was not followed with the other subsidized housing projects in the community. As indicated in Table 4—3, only three of the seventeen subsidized housing projects in the seven new communities were isolated from the rest of the community—the single-family subdivisions in Jonathan and Forest Park and the large planned unit development (PUD) in Park Forest. However, the size of the PUD and its amenities made it almost imperative that it be set off from other units.

Federal Housing Administration (FHA) standards and restrictions had a significant impact on the design and spatial location of many of the subsidized housing projects. Reston, for example, had the only concentration of several projects in one area—three garden apartment complexes located in one village. FHA approved the sites in spite of resident concern that the nearest elementary school would be impacted by the large number of children from low- and moderate-income families. However, these projects were within walking distance of the new United States Geological Survey facility in Reston and near the most expensive single-family neighborhood in the community.

Rental costs and purchase prices of the subsidized housing units were controlled by FHA (see Table 4—4 for a description of each of the subsidy programs). Cost criteria, perforce, caused the quality of the units to be somewhat below that of the nonsubsidized units in the communities. However, the majority of the subsidized housing was not an eyesore. Some of the projects, like the large PUD in Park Forest built with Illinois Housing Development Authority funds, were of excellent architectural quality.

The subsidized housing units tended also not to be spatially isolated from facilities and services in the communities (see Table 4—5). There was little difference in distance from schools for the lower or higher income residents. The same were true for shopping facilities. Recreational facilities were slightly closer for residents of the subsidized housing. The effect of these location factors on residents' satisfaction with their communities and quality of life is analyzed in Chapter 7.

Table 4-3.   Subsidized Housing Projects in Sample Communities

Community	Number of Units	Subsidy Program[a]	Initial Occupancy	Percent Minority Population	Spatial Location and Design
Columbia	300	FHA 221(d)3	1969	30	Townhouse apartments on five sites in two villages
	10	FHA 235	1970	NR	Single-family; scattered; one village
	108[e]	FHA 236	1971	48	Garden apartments; one site; near village center
	12	FHA 235	1971	NR	Townhouses; in project of 156 units
	100[e]	FHA 236	1973	35[d]	High-rise apartments; across from village center
Reston	198[e]	FHA 221(d)3	1969	17	Garden apartments; nine buildings; one site
	138[e]	FHA 202	1971	2	High-rise apartments; elderly; near village center
	240	FHA 236	1973	20	Garden apartments; fourteen buildings; one site
	200	FHA 236	1974	NR	Garden apartments; twelve buildings; one site
	50	Turnkey	1974	NR	Garden apartments; one site
Jonathan	55	FHA 235	1971	0	Single-family; entire subdivision; isolated
	96[e]	FHA 236	1971	3	Townhouse apartments; one site
Forest Park	201	FHA 235	1971	10	Single-family; entire subdivision; isolated
Park Forest	106	FHA 213	1971	2	High-rise apartments; elderly; near town center
	248	IHDA[b]	1973	10	High-rise apartments and townhouses; 372-unit mixed-income PUD; isolated
Park Forest South	46	IHDA[c]	1974	NR	Existing, unoccupied high-rise apartment building in four-building complex (converted to FHA Section 236)

| Lake Havasu City | 64 | FHA 235 | 1969 | 0 | Single-family; 50 percent of subdivision |

Note: Projects as of December 1973.   NR = Not reported.

[a] See Table 4–4 for a description of these subsidy programs.

[b] Illinois Housing Development Authority; 66 percent of units financed under FHA Section 236 program.

[c] Illinois Housing Development Authority; 78 percent of units financed under FHA Section 236 program.

[d] Based on prerent-up applications.

[e] Low-income rent-supplement units included in projects.

Table 4—4. Housing Subsidy Programs

Type of Program	Year Established	Purpose	Subsidy	Income Limits[a]
Section 202	1959	To make loans to non-profit or limited profit sponsors, cooperatives, and public agencies for lower middle income persons. (Program converted to Section 236 in 1969).	Below-market interest rate loans of 3 percent for sponsors; tax incentives through rapid depreciation.	$5670 for one person; $6345 for two persons (Reston Interfaith limits).
Housing for the elderly or handicapped; rental or cooperative; construction rehabilitation or improvement.				
Section 221 (d)(3)	1961	To insure loans for rental or cooperative housing (similar to Section 236).	Below-market interest rates (3 percent in 1971); tax incentives through depreciation. (Phased out in favor of Section 236 program.)	$5700 for family of one to $9350 for families of five or six (Columbia Interfaith limits).
Construction or rehabilitation of dwelling with 5 or more units for low- and moderate-income families.				
Section 236	1968	To insure loans in order to reduce rent for families with up to 135 percent of public housing income admission level.	Interest reduction payments that reduce interest rate to as little as 1 percent; tax incentives through rapid depreciation.	$5500 to $11,000.
Rental and cooperative housing assistance for construction or rehabilitation of 5 or more units.				

Section 235 Home ownership subsidy for moderate-income families; newly constructed, rehabilitated or existing single-family (including cooperatives). Option of builder to convert to Section 235 when eligible purchaser is processed.	1968	To insure loans for families with incomes up to 135 percent of public housing income admission level.	Reduction of interest rate to as little as 1 percent depending on income. (Mortgage limits: $18,000; or $21,000 in high-cost areas; $200 down; 35 years. Up to $3000 can be added for property consisting of four bedrooms for families of five or more.)	Approximately same as Section 236. Assets cannot exceed $2000, including mortgage or share of mortgage payment for one year.
Turnkey Private builder finds site and builds units for local housing authority after it approves plans. Authority buys units from builder and uses them for low-rent housing as in conventional programs.	1965	Same as conventional rental programs; results in faster construction.	Financing and local tax subsidies are the same as conventional programs, but initiative and administration during construction handled by builders rather than housing authorities.	$5444 for one person to $8000 for eight persons (Reston Turnkey Units). Somewhat above public housing limits.
Section 101 Rent supplements	1965	To subsidize rents for low-income families who are displaced, elderly, handicapped, or living in substandard housing damaged by natural disasters.	Difference between gross rent and 25 percent of tenants' income paid to owner on behalf of lower income tenants.	Not applicable.

Table 4–4. continued overleaf . . . .

Table 4—4. continued

Type of Program	Year Established	Purpose	Subsidy	Income Limits[a]
Section 231	1959	To insure loans for rental housing designed for elderly and handicapped.	None	$2000 to $8000 (Public housing limits in Chicago area).
Operation Breakthrough	1969	To award contracts for experimental production, marketing and management projects to improve housing process.	Outlays of $49 million; includes Section 1010 (technological advancement).	Not applicable.
Illinois Housing Development Authority	1967	To serve the needs of moderate- to middle-income families not previously included in federal government programs. (Inclusion of some Section 236 subsidies extends the income range served by IHDA developments; application procedures for subsidies under Section 236 are streamlined.)	Low-interest loans for construction and permanent mortgage financing through sale of tax exempt bonds. Section 236 interest-assistance payments can be allocated to some of the units.	$8000 to $17,000.

Section 23

| Public housing leasing. Local housing authority leases existing units from owners (or new ones built for this purpose) at market rental rates and subleases to low-income households at lower rents—absorbing differences as a subsidy. | 1965 | To provide opportunity for eligible households to locate appropriate existing units. | Federal government pays difference up to amount per unit it would contribute in conventional public housing program. Housing allowance paid to renter (the housing authority) rather than the occupant. | Public housing. |

[a]Income limits vary by size of family and region. Unless otherwise specified, the figures cited are an approximation of extreme limits. The low figure is for a one-person family. For example, in the Chicago area a six-person family with an income of $8,910 can qualify for housing under Section 236; a one-person family is limited to $6075. In Howard County, Maryland, the limits are $8775 and $5535, respectively.

Table 4-5. Median Distance to Nearest Facilities for Residents Living in Subsidized and Nonsubsidized Housing *(distance in miles)*

	New Communities[a]		Conventional Communities
Facility	Nonsubsidized Housing	Subsidized Housing	Subsidized Housing
Elementary school	0.74	0.68	0.38
Middle school	2.27	3.14	2.48
High school	1.97	1.70	4.26
Park or playground	0.30	0.02	0.21
Neighborhood/community shopping center	1.06	0.87	0.78
Supermarket	0.98	0.76	1.02
Convenience store	1.19	1.40	0.63
Bicycling/walking path	0.30	0.19	2.46
Swimming facility	0.83	0.76	2.94
Hospital	8.92	8.64	5.17
Doctor	1.19	1.42	1.31
Public health clinic	4.17	3.79	18.90

[a]Figures are for: Columbia, Reston, Forest Park, Lake Havasu City and Jonathan. Because of the sampling time frame, Park Forest and Park Forest South are not included.

RESIDENT HETEROGENEITY

Does the provision of subsidized housing guarantee class mix in a community, even on a macro-level? The data in Table 4-6 indicate that it does. Four categories of residents are represented in the table—those in segregated communities, higher income residents (nonsubsidized) in integrated communities, and residents of subsidized housing in the new and conventional communities.[c]

As the data indicate, the higher income residents of both the integrated and segregated communities were demographically similar. They held similar positions, had about the same education, and family composition was identical. Even with the same education and occupational indexes, however, those in the integrated communities earned about $2500 less annually. These characteristics are pointed out in order to show that the middle and upper class residents in the integrated communities were not unique.

The demographics of the residents of the subsidized housing in the conventional communities are presented for the same reasons. Race was the only characteristic in which there was a significant dif-

[c]See Appendix A for the location and a description of the conventional communities with subsidized housing.

ference. On an aggregate level, there were almost 34 percent more whites in the subsidized housing in the new communities.

The residents of subsidized housing account, on the average, for about 9 percent of the population of their host communities. From the data in Table 4–6, it is more than evident that they represented a lower socioeconomic status. They differed dramatically from their middle and upper class neighbors. They held much lower status jobs. With larger families, they earned less than half the annual income, had less education, and more of the households had female household heads. In addition, residents of subsidized housing spent proportionately more of their income on housing. The higher income residents' home value was approximately two times their annual income; for residents of subsidized housing it was three times. Also striking was the difference in rent. Residents of subsidized housing spent approximately 18 percent of their income on rent; higher income residents about 13 percent.

In sum, while the demographic mix of the host metropolitan areas was not matched, a socioeconomic mix occurred in seven of the new communities. The next chapter distinguishes among the factors in the development process that facilitated this integration.

Table 4—6. Demographic Characteristics of New Community and Subsidized Housing Residents

Characteristic	New Communities		Subsidized Housing	
	No Subsidized Housing[a]	With Subsidized Housing[b]	New Communities	Conventional Communities
Occupation of Household Head (percent)				
Professional	34	35	15	12
Manager-administrator	24	26	9	8
Sales	14	10	5	3
Clerical	7	5	13	15
Craftsman	14	12	25	21
Operatives	3	4	16	19
Laborers	<1	1	7	8
Service workers	4	5	10	14
Occupational Index[c] (median)	620	610	339	325
Income—Family (percent)				
Less than $5,000	3	6	16	24
$5,000—$9,999	8	11	46	36
$10,000—$12,499	9	14	19	19
$12,500—$14,999	12	13	7	11
$15,000—$17,499	16	12	4	4
$17,500—$19,999	13	12	4	4
$20,000—$24,999	20	15	3	2
$25,000—$29,999	9	8	2	0
$30,000—$39,999	7	5	0	1
$40,000—$49,999	2	2	0	0
$50,000 or more	2	1	0	0
Median income	$18,800	$16,300	$7,500	$7,500

Education				
Median number of years—				
household head	14.0	14.6	12.4	12.0
Household head and spouse (percent)				
Neither BA	48	44	87	91
Either BA	32	29	10	7
Both BA	20	27	3	2
Median Home Value	$37,500	$37,500	$22,500	$22,500
Median Rent	$189	$183	$113	$103
Race (percent)				
White	96	93	82	48
Black	3	6	17	51
Other	1	1	1	1
Number in Household (mean)				
Total	3.3	3.3	4.0	4.6
Children	1.3	1.3	2.2	2.7
Female Headed Households (percent)	1	11	24	24
Household Head Employed within Community (percent)	10	14[d]	25[d]	19
Sample Size	1,997	883	271	243

[a] Because of sampling time frame, figures include residents of Park Forest and Park Forest South.
[b] Does not include subsidized housing subsample.
[c] Dunan SEI—rescaled for 1970 census.
[d] Excludes Lake Havasu City—a freestanding new community—where approximately 94 percent of the residents worked in community.

Chapter 5

Economic and Class Integration:
The Development Process

If indeed, integration exists, why only in the seven new communities and not in the others? What accounts for the variance between the two sets of communities? Several disparate hypotheses have been offered and they are evaluated in this chapter.

HYPOTHESES

A "New Breed" of Developer
During the early 1960s, two community-level proposals were widely advocated.[a] One was a strategy for strengthening the ghetto through support of black capitalism. The other has been described as an idea which promised to "... reconcile the goals of social contribution with the profit motive. Spawned by a mixture of idealistic concepts and real estate concomics, the 'new town'—long an ideal of urban philosophers—started to take shape as a viable market innovation" (Mahlon Apgar IV 1971, p. 90). The developers of these communities are a "new breed," who enter "... the field with a special sense of mission which few merchant builders hold." The claim is that this sense of mission inspires a unique product—a "total environment ... with every consideration planned in advance in a complete new city" (Edward P. Eichler and Marshal Kaplan 1970, pp. 36–37).

[a]For a critique of the two community-level proposals, see Jeanne R. Lowe (1969).

Government Intervention

All developers of new communities are ultimately guided by the profit motive. And because of return on investment per unit, housing supplied by the private market largely serves the needs of middle- and upper-income groups. Hence, only through government imposed requirements, such as fair share plans, and court decisions, or through large incentives, such as water and sewer grants, will private developers provide housing for low- and moderate-income families.[b]

Another facilitator of integration is the federal new communities program, which offers incentive, in the form of grants, in return for social mix. Thus, communities participating in the program will be more likely to provide for economic, class and racial mix.

Demographics of the Area

Because of the often-given warning that class and racial mix are very difficult to achieve concomitantly, it is theorized that it is easier to achieve economic and class integration in areas where the number of nonwhites is small.

Geographical Location

In certain regions of the country people are more receptive to the notion of integration and there is enough of a market to support those communities that choose to integrate. On the other hand, it is impossible to attempt integration in areas that are socially conservative.

Providing Amenities

By offering services and facilities not usually provided by communities, developers might be able to entice residents who would not ordinarily move into an integrated community. The community would be more attractive, if the financial burden for the amenities is not heavy for the consumer.[c]

Developer's Perception of the Market

If a developer believes that an integrated community can be marketed, the community will successfully integrate. The key is the developer's analysis of the market.

---

[b]According to Ruchelman and Brownstein (1973, p. 3), the public and private sector differ in policy objectives because they have different consituencies: "The constituency of private decision-makers is usually narrowly based as defined by market goals. The constituency of public decision-makers is more broadly based, covering a wide range of public concerns. Public decision-makers, moreover, must keep a wary eye on citizen feedback and are subject to pressures from a variety of interest groups."

[c]See Gans (1973, pp. 148–151) for a discussion of this and other policies for macro-integration.

Seller's Market

Since most people prefer homogeneous communities, the developer should build where there is a scarcity of housing. People will then be forced to move into integrated communities.

Resident Recruitment

Information about the integrated nature of the community should be made available to prospective buyers, so that those most hostile toward integration will locate somewhere else. In addition, when the low-income families move into the community, there will be less resentment because residents are not surprised.

Macro- versus Micro-integration

It is easier to integrate on a macro- rather than on a micro- level. Low-income families should be concentrated in neighborhoods or blocks to minimize contact with higher income residents, who will accept this form of integration more readily.

A corollary to this is that developers should use subsidy programs that do not require income mix within the projects.

Timing

Although the developer should advertise the integrated nature of the community, housing for low-income families should be built only after part of the community is settled by higher income residents.

Adjacent Classes

It is easier to integrate where there is not a great disparity between the classes.

Raising the Issue

In older communities, developers should try to keep the building of housing for low-income people from becoming a public issue. If more people become involved, it is less likely that housing will be approved.[d]

INTEGRATION STRATEGIES

The analysis below of the strategies utilized to create either integrated or segregated communities will show that the key to successful

[d]Studies of the fluoridation issue show that where the issue came to a vote, it lost about two of three times, often despite support from public health officers. The most successful route was through the support of a mayor or manager, and thus by administrative action rather than by popular vote. See Robert L. Crain, Elihu Katz and Donald B. Rosenthal (1967).

integration is the developer's perception of the market. The reality is that no two developers may view the market in the same way. In fact, markets are created. If a developer believes that an integrated community can be marketed, he can plan for it by informing residents, providing amenities and facilitating implementation. If subsidies are also available, housing for low-income families can be provided.

For the purpose of evaluating the hypotheses, the new communities are divided into four categories: (1) those that planned for integration and were successful—Columbia, Reston and Jonathan; (2) those that did not plan for mix, but were integrated—Forest Park, Park Forest and Lake Havasu City; (3) those that attempted mix, but as of the spring of 1973 had not achieved it—Irvine and Park Forest South;[e] and (4) those that had no integration goals and as a result were homogeneous—Laguna Niguel, Foster City, Westlake Village, North Palm Beach and Elk Grove Village.

Integrated Communities: Perception of the Market, Planning for Integration and Resident Recruitment

Columbia. While many communities consider economic mix an anathema, part of Columbia's credibility nationally is based on its residential heterogeneity. James Rouse was the first new community developer to begin to operationalize socioeconomic goals and facilitate their attainment. He saw housing for lower income families as necessary for a "complete and balanced city." He viewed balance in terms of three dimensions: housing and employment mix; activity and service mix; and demographic and life-style mix ("Report to the Columbia Task Force on a 'Balance Community' and the Commitment to 10% Subsidized Housing in Columbia, Maryland" 1971). Rouse originally conceived of subsidized housing as nonprofit, community owned and serving as a kind of "halfway house" for young people moving up.

Rouse's objective of socioeconomic integration in Columbia was not a systematically based philosophy, but a community-based rationale tied to the goal of self-sufficiency of the city: "houses and apartments at rents and prices to match the incomes of all who will work there, from the company janitor to company executive" has become part of Columbia's rhetoric (Richard O. Brooks and John Bordes 1972, p. 2).

[e]Although Table 4–3 lists Park Forest South as having forty-six units of subsidized housing, these units were still being processed at the time of this study. In addition, attempts at building more units in the community had failed.

Two of the people Rouse hired in key planning positions, Robert Finely and Morton Hoppenfield, were drawn from the public sector. They had backgrounds in public service and had demonstrated a commitment to the "general welfare."[f] It was Morton Hoppenfield, the man selected to design the city, who suggested that a study group of social scientists and economists be created. A series of workshops were held during the summer and fall of 1963. Out of these sessions came reports on the feasibility of attaining social goals and strategies for implementation. There were, however, conflicting proposals concerning the provision of housing for low- and moderate-income families. The Columbia Economic Model produced a *need* figure of 10 percent low- and moderate-income housing, but confirmed a policy of rejection of that provision in Columbia. Based on a market analysis, Robert Gladstone suggested delaying implementation (Robert Gladstone and Associates 1964); and Herbert J. Gans noted the potential dangers in delay and detailed tactics for implementation (1968, pp. 183–201).

As soon as plans for the community began to be formalized, Rouse announced that the major strategy to be employed for achieving a balanced community "is to set aside a minimum of ten percent of all dwelling units in Columbia for low and middle income housing." The process began when Rouse contacted church groups who were in the midst of organizing into an ecumenical council. He suggested that they sponsor the first subsidized housing project, Interfaith Housing.[g]

[f]See Eichler and Kaplan (1970, p. 63) for the backgrounds of Hoppenfield and Finley.

[g]The Interfaith Housing Task Force was established in 1966, soon after construction began in Columbia. The task force grew out of the coalition of church groups. With a $25,000 grant from the Catholic Archdiocese of Baltimore and another $18,000 commited by the Columbia Cooperative Ministry, the task force began studying the feasibility of providing low-cost housing in the community. The study resulted in a recommendation for a subsidized housing development to be scattered in Columbia's first village and suggestions for integrating the residents into the social and economic life of the community.

From the inception of the task force, James Rouse supported its goals and provided consultants for the project. With guarantees of continued support from the developer, the task force incorporated (Interfaith Housing Corporation) and applied for assistance under FHA Section 231(d)(3), the only subsidy program available at the time. Approval took a considerable amount of time. Interfaith was the first subsidized moderate-income project that the FHA office in Baltimore had handled. To complicate matters it was also the first subsidized housing project of any kind in Howard County, and for a time the county commissioners refused to cooperate in granting approval and authorizing water and sewer taps. In spite of all of these problems, groundbreaking took place in the spring of 1968. By late 1970, 300 units, scattered on five sites in two villages, had been completed.

Rouse also institued several policies and programs which ultimately had a synergistic effect on socioeconomic integration. One of the most important actions was to advertise widely the social goals of the community. This included not only mention of the 10 percent low- and moderate-income housing objective, but also strong emphasis on the fact that the community was to be racially open. This latter goal was underlined by the inclusion of blacks in advertising and by staffing the information booth with both whites and blacks. A sliding scale for land prices was also established, with up to a 50 percent reduction for builders of housing for low- and moderate-income families.

Rouse's in-house economists and market analysts had determined that it would be most feasible to build lower cost housing after one-third of the community had been developed. However, they also felt that if a developer is honest about commitments, the lower priced housing should be built from the beginning. The conflict was resolved when it took over two years to get final approval for the Interfaith project. In the end, Rouse followed Gladstone's advice to offer only middle-income housing in the first two years, with lower priced units offered only after market experience had been gained.

With 7 percent of the dwelling units in Columbia under subsidy programs when this study was conducted,[h] Rouse had fallen short of

[h]The other subsidized housing projects in Columbia are discussed below. For more details see Appendix B. *Howard Homes.* In order to provide home ownership for moderate-income families, the owners of Howard Homes were asked by James Rouse to come to Columbia as a joint venture. In 1968 more than 150 units were built—selling for $14,750 to $16,950. FHA allocated funds so that forty units could be sold under FHA Section 235. Only twelve people qualified; the rest of the units were sold under FHA Section 203 conventional financing. Thirty-four of these units had a third-floor "piggy-back," rent controlled apartment that could not be rented for more than $99 a month for five years. One of the motivations for the joint venture was to control home values. In 1974 some of these townhouses were selling for over $30,000.

Ryland Homes. In order to provide even more home ownership for moderate-income families, Rouse, in 1970, convinced Ryland Homes to construct homes which sold for $19,990 to $23,900. FHA authorized fifty of these homes for FHA Section 235 mortgages. However, because of a first-come-first-served policy, only ten families qualified before all of the homes had been sold. In 1974 these homes were selling for close to double their original cost.

Copperstone Circle. In its planning stages Copperstone was not intended to be a subsidized project. Copperstone is owned by Columbia Development Corporation (CDC) and was built by Rouse-Wates Company, both subsidiaries of the Howard Research and Development Corporation. Approval for FHA Section 236 subsidy took only six months and the 108-unit complex was completed in less than one year. While Interfaith Corporation paid half of the market rate for its land, Copperstone Circle costs were computed at $450 per unit below market rate. If effect, the Copperstone site was merely a transfer of property on paper.

Abbott House. Abbott House was proposed by the Rouse-Wates Company as a demonstration project under an Operation Breakthrough grant. Construction of this 100-unit mid-rise was delayed several times. However, once it received FHA Section 236 approval in 1972, construction proceeded rapidly.

his stated goal of 10 percent low- and moderate-income housing. Land and construction costs and the moratorium on federal subsidies were making it increasingly difficult to reach the goal. A Rouse-Wates proposal for 160 units in the Village of Locust Park was caught in the 1973 Federal subsidized housing moritorium.

Several suggestions have been made and methods attempted in order to catch up. The developer encouraged builders to construct low-cost housing by not counting these units in the overall density of their projects. There also was an attempt by JWR, the mortgage banking subsidiary of the Rouse organization, to design a second-mortgage plan which would allow moderate-income families to purchase homes without federal subsidies. In the Village of Owen Brown, Howard Homes[i] built eighteen less expensive models in the 150-unit Greenleaf development under a new Maryland State mortgage program. These units were available to moderate-income families earning between $9200 and $11,000 a year. Prior to public announcements, the availability of the units was made known to residents of the subsidized rental housing in Columbia.

As mentioned above, James Rouse's goals were community based —a vague objective of a self-sufficient city. At the early planning sessions, the projected price distribution of homes and resident income distributions were based on regional profiles, suburban profiles, normal profiles and other sophisticated analyses developed within the framework of the Columbia Economic Model.[j] However, there is little question that the key influencing factor on all economic integration policies was the manifest commitment of the developer, James W. Rouse. The Rouse Company or its subsidiaries not only initiated the construction of a majority of the subsidized housing units in the community, but perhaps more important, the developer made a number of crucial decisions which will ease future acceptance of both racial and economic integration.

Rouse, in effect, created a community with a nonexclusionary ethos. Important actions that facilitated the provision of low-cost housing in Columbia included: (1) the recruitment of key personnel who also had a commitment to socioeconomic integration; (2) early solicitation of strategies for implementation of economic integration objectives; (3) early announcements of economic and racial integration goals; (4) inclusion of goals in advertisement of the community; (5) facilitating the construction of low-cost housing by writing down

[i]The joint venture partnership between Howard Homes and the Rouse organization was dissolved in order to allow Howard Homes to build in other areas.

[j]See Brooks and Bordes (1972) for a description of the economic and social planning of the work-group sessions.

the cost of land; (6) development of alternate strategies for the provision of low-cost housing; and (7) working with organizations and residents of the community to establish the credibility of economic integration policies.

Reston.   Like Columbia, Reston is often cited as an example of a successfully integrated community. There are parallels between the policies of the two communities; but, there are also important differences.

The most obvious variation is that Reston has had two developers. Robert E. Simon, Jr., the original developer, did not formalize his concern for social structure in Reston, as Rouse did in Columbia. Through his actions, however, he made it known that it should ". . . be possible for any who want to remain in this single community to do so throughout their lives. Changes in circumstances of age, family composition, or financial situation should not make uprooting inevitable or even preferable" (quoted in Eichler and Kaplan 1970, p. 80).

Although all of the subsidized housing in Reston was constructed after the Gulf Oil Corporation took over control of the community, many of Simon's actions facilitated its existence. He set precedents that Gulf-Reston, Inc., followed, often at the insistence of the residents.[k]

[k]The subsidized housing projects in Reston are listed below. For more details see Appendix B. *Cedar-Ridge.* Cedar Ridge was already in the planning stages when Gulf came into the community. Partly because of resident pressure through the Reston Community Association (RCA), which was formed in 1967 as a vehicle for influencing county government, the new developer felt obligated to complete it. FHA granted the request for FHA Section 221(d)(3) funds partially on the basis of Fairfax County's need. The 198-unit complex was completed in 1969 and remains under the management of Cedar-Ridge Properties, a subsidiary of Gulf-Reston.
Fellowship House. Simon envisioned housing for the elderly in each of the village centers. To that end, in 1964 he suggested that a Methodist church group sponsor a project. However, by the time the group received approval from their state organization, a Lutheran church group had decided to sponsor an elderly complex across from Lake Anne Village Center. Land was sold to the Lutherans for $1000 per unit instead of the market value of $4000. The sponsors originally wanted to build a 200-unit complex, but FHA would only approve half that number. Simon agreed to continue an option on more land at the same cost. Gulf-Reston followed with the same type of cooperation with the project. The 138-unit high-rise building was completed in 1971 under the FHA Section 202 subsidy program.
Fellowship House II. FHA officials later admitted having made a mistake in not approving 200 units in 1970; at that time they felt there was no market. Fellowship II will now cost twice as much as it would have if built as part of the original plans. Since the FHA Section 202 program has been discontinued, there are added legal and building difficulties in matching FHA Section 236 construc-

The economic and class integration planning process in Reston was considerably more pluralistic than that in Columbia. This was a result in part of the two developers and the fact that after the first subsidized housing project—Cedar-Ridge—Gulf-Reston decided not to sponsor any more projects itself.

Actual housing need for families with low and moderate incomes was considered in making many of the decisions in Reston, especially by FHA. The factors considered in determining housing need included the income level of the employees of approximately 100 firms located in Reston, the Dulles Airport facility located nearby, and the new USGS headquarters. It was estimated that 600 of the 2800 employees of USGS would earn $8000 per year or less. There was a paucity of low- and moderate-income housing in the county. This was especially a problem because Fairfax County had the highest

---

tion to the older building. At the time of this study, ground had not yet been broken for the addition.

Fox-Mill. Fox Mill is owned and sponsored by Hans Schultz, the construction company that built Cedar-Ridge. Gulf-Reston sold the land to Schultz for $1400 per unit. If it were a market rate project, the cost would have been $3400. There were some problems in getting the project approved by the county and delays due to lack of FHA funds. The 240-unit project was completed in 1973.

Laurel Glade. The planning for what eventually became Laurel Glade began in 1968. The Baptist Church in Reston decided there was enough elderly housing under consideration for the community. It envisioned housing for the employees of the proposed United States Geological Survey (USGS) headquarters. Other groups became involved and were incorporated into Interfaith Housing Corporation.

This project has a history of difficulties. The original consultant did not follow through on its commitments to Interfaith. It was decided that there would be a greater chance of success if Interfaith entered into a joint venture with Conrad Cafritz Company for sponsorship. As a result, Housing America took over the planning in 1972.

Site and cost negotiations with Gulf-Reston took almost five years and involved getting a zoning variance from the county. Interfaith ultimately purchased the land from Gulf at $1500 per unit. This price and other cost increases necessitated getting approval from FHA for exceptional limits.

Interfaith applied for FHA Section 236 funds in September 1971. After initial approval, FHA cancelled the project in the summer of 1972. The Home Opportunities Council of Washington (HOC) and the Reston Community Association (RCA) filed a complaint with FHA because the site for Laurel Glade was located near Fox-Mill and another low-rent apartment complex. RCA and HOC felt that this configuration would lead to a concentration of children from low- and moderate-income families in one elementary school. In response, Gulf-Reston held a meeting to defend the project's location. The regional director of FHA was very impressed with the presentation and the Laurel Glade project received its commitment three months later. At the time of this study, the project was under construction.

"Turnkey." Fairfax County Housing and Redevelopment Authority sponsored fifty units for families whose income level was just above those who could qualify for public housing. The county first approached Gulf-Reston with a proposal in 1970; the contract was signed in August 1972. The garden units were under construction at the time of this study.

per capita income in the nation. Median home value in the county as a whole was about $48,000, with median monthly rent $240.

Soon after Gulf took control of Reston, a new marketing study was completed which recommended that no more low- or moderate-income housing be built. Again, partly due to citizen influence, Gulf chose to ignore the findings. The former president of Gulf-Reston said that Gulf-Reston "had to fulfill Simon's commitment."

Gulf also continued the policy of writing down the cost of land to sponsors of low-cost housing. Land subsidies thus far have amounted to $1087 million. Other measures of Gulf-Reston's commitment to socioeconomic integration include its decision not to challenge Fairfax County's Housing Allocation Plan and its unsuccessful proposal to HUD for provision of low-cost homes in exchange for open space grants.

The sponsors of the various projects in Reston felt that Gulf-Reston had been cooperative and had facilitated the implementation of their plans. Gulf-Reston also continued to advertise the economic and social mix in the community.[l] It was only after citizen pressure and a complaint filed with HUD,[m] however, that Gulf-Reston began to use minorities in its advertisements and as tour guides.

Jonathan. Jonathan was the first community in the country to receive a loan guarantee under Title IV of the 1968 Housing and Urban Development Act. Under its project agreement (1970, p. 17) with the federal government, Jonathan Development Corporation (JDC) was required to,

---

Tall Oaks Towers. Not all proposals for subsidized housing in Reston were successful. As mentioned above, the Methodists were first approached by Simon to sponsor a project for the elderly. After they finally received permission to proceed and got an option on a site across the street from their church, FHA discouraged the proposal.

Because the history of nonprofit sponsors is dismal, the Methodists (now incorporated into Redeemer Housing Corporation) entered into a limited partnership with Shelter Corporation of Minnesota. A new application was filed in April 1972. Meetings and negotiations with FHA over the number of apartments and other criteria lasted months. An option on land was finally agreed upon with Gulf ($1500 per unit) and the county approved funds for water and sewer taps. Finally, FHA approved the project over exceptional cost limits. The proposal then got caught in the moratorium. The option on the land then ran out, but the nine-year history of this project was not quite over. The sponsors continued to explore the possibility of state financing under a new Virginia statute.

[l]The brochure *Inside Reston, Virginia* proudly states: "Today, Reston provides housing to meet the needs, tastes and income levels of everyone desiring to live here. . . . Reston was the first to offer retired citizens and families with low and moderate incomes the benefits of living in an American new town."

[m]The Housing Opportunities Council of Washington filed a complaint with HUD charging Reston with violation of the 1968 Civil Rights Act—use of minority models in advertisements and use of the equal housing logo.

... provide a planning framework which will encourage people of all ethnic, social and economic backgrounds to settle in the Project. ... To this end the Developer shall use its best efforts to achieve the schedule of production of housing for low and moderate income persons and families.

According to the president of Jonathan Development Corporation, it was always in the plans to match the demographic profile of the metropolitan area. He reported that Henry McKnight was committed to this goal, even if JDC had not received a federal guarantee.[n]

Many of the decisions about subsidized housing in Jonathan were made informally. The late Senator McKnight was a friend of the president of Dreyfus Interstate Development Corporation, the builders of both of the subsidized housing projects in the community, and initial contacts and negotiations between the two were informal. Dreyfus had built over 3000 subsidized housing units in other parts of the country and looked to involvement in Jonathan as a means of establishing a foothold in Minnesota.[o]

The Jonathan Development Corporation followed through on its commitment to economic and class integration. McKnight encouraged Dreyfus Interstate Development Corporation to build the subsidized single-family homes by writing down the cost of the land and entered into a joint venture with the builder of the multifamily housing. Both of these developments were included in JDC's advertisements.

The plan is that it will be a balanced community in all respects. The federal government has initiated major programs to assist persons in lower income brackets to rent or buy proper housing for their families. Some of the homes and apartments in Jonathan qualify for the federal purchase or rental assistance programs (Jonathan Development Corporation, n.d.).

[n]There is some question, however, whether JDC would have gone ahead with the development of the community without the federal guarantee.

[o]The two subsidized projects in Jonathan are described below. For more details see Appendix B. *Farmhill Townhouses*. JDC and Dreyfus entered into a limited partnership for the development of Farmhill. Originally, Dreyfus wanted the project to be a cooperative, but eventually decided to apply for FHA Section 236 subsidy. The 96-unit complex was completed in 1971.

Neighborhood 5. As in the arrangement for Farmhill, Dreyfus relied on JDC to do whatever market analysis was necessary and to select the site. JDC wrote down the cost of the land for these single-family homes from $4000 to $2700 per lot. At the same time, Dreyfus built another subdivision of similar homes, but with garages and on larger lots, in a nearby section of the community. FHA officials reported that they wanted to scatter the subsidized housing units throughout the community, but ran into opposition to this proposal from a key member of the JDC staff. Later there was general agreement that the FHA suggestion for scattering subsidized housing would have had a more positive impact on future policy decisions.

Other measures of JDC's commitment to providing housing for low- and moderate-income families include the fact that it brought in some moderate-income housing without federal subsidies and that proposals were made to HUD for other alternate means of providing low-cost housing (Letter to Secretary James Lynn, Department of Housing and Urban Development, June 21, 1973).

Integrated Communities: Perception of the Market, Not Planning for Integration and Resident Recruitment

The developers of Park Forest, Forest Park and Lake Havasu City did not plan for economic integration. Nor did they conceive of their communities as exclusionary. Early decisions were made which, in the long run, facilitated the acceptance of low-cost housing.

The developers of these communities encouraged the construction of homes to capture the middle range of the housing market and did not advertise their communities solely with an appeal to higher income consumers. In addition, both Forest Park and Park Forest are racially integrated. Residents moved into the communities with that awareness and early residents remained after the communities integrated. All of these factors contributed to the nonexclusionary ethos of these communities.

Village of Park Forest.   As mentioned in Chapter 3 the relatively low-cost dwelling units built around the large shopping center in Park Forest were seen as a way to provide customers for the businesses. The concepts of a planned community and a regional shopping center were quite innovative in 1948, and people moved to the community knowing that they were involved with a unique community. This uniqueness continued to be evident in the resulting social composition of the community.

Racial integration occurred because of the persistence of several residents in the community.[p] It was not the policy of the developers in the late 1940s or early 1950s to sell homes to blacks (or Asians). The entire community was not supportive either. As a reaction to the

---

[p]Beginning in 1949, the fight for racial integration in Park Forest was led by Harry Teshima. One of the first residents in the community, Mr. Teshima was renting and wanted to buy one of the tract homes. After the developer refused to sell in the tract development, it was agreed that a custom lot could be purchased. The rationale was that there was less chance of hurting sales in the custom lot area. In the beginning Teshima and a few other local residents worked for integration without the benefit of fair housing laws or civil rights workers. The biggest assist came from the depressed housing market. Twenty-five years later, Mr. Teshima was still involved in integration efforts in the South Chicago area.

first black family moving in, a White Citizens' League was formed in 1959. After the League's extreme stand became evident to other residents, it was forced to disband. The village board, while not actively encouraging integration efforts at first, worked to protect the rights of early black residents and eventually became an advocate.

By the time the first subsidized housing project was proposed in 1969,[q] the community had developed a reputation as being open and liberal. Residents, who were predominantly well educated and middle class, were aware that they did not live in a homogeneous community and worked to bring about a more heterogeneous one.[r]

Acceptance of public housing—Juniper Towers—was facilitated by the characteristics of the clientele group—elderly persons, some of whom were former residents of the community. The fact that the

[q]The two subsidized housing projects in Park Forest are described below. For more details see Appendix B. *Juniper Towers.* The idea for a senior citizens' project began in 1969 when the village became aware of a Cook County Housing Authority (CCHA) development in a nearby community. The two senior citizens' organizations in Park Forest at the time encouraged the planning. To determine interest and need the village conducted a survey, which underestimated need but was credible enough to pursue plans. First HUD was contacted about the possibility of receiving public housing funds. It was finally decided that CCHA could obtain a subsidy more readily. CCHA applied for the funds and hired the architects and the builders. The 106-unit, high-rise structure was completed in 1971. The site had been deeded to the village by the developer for park land. However, the developer readily agreed to a change in the convenant so the site could be turned over to the CCHA.

Arbor Trails. The site on which the Arbor Trails project is located was only recently annexed by Park Forest. Jack Telander, the builder and sponsor, had owned the land for over ten years, originally planning to develop it into a large-lot, custom-home subdivision. However, after conducting a market survey of the area in 1971, Telander concluded that the only profitable venture would be multi-family housing for moderate-income families. Telander, who also built Juniper Towers, contacted the Illinois Housing Development Authority (IHDA) for funding and received immediate approval.

IHDA provided financing for moderate-income developments below market rate and allowed not more than 40 percent of the units to be subsidized under FHA Section 236. Monies from bonds floated on a statewide level were supplemented with FHA Section 236 subsidies. Because of this method of financing, IHDA townhouses and apartments offered better construction and a wide range of amenities not usually available under straight federal subsidy programs.

There was no real concern by the village board over the fact that Arbor Trails was going to be a subsidized project. There was no discussion of the type of people who would be residents or the impact of a nonelderly subsidized housing project on the community by the board or by other residents in the community. Information about IHDA is available in Illinois Housing Development Authority (1971).

[r]In 1971 a group of citizens announced the formation of the Park Forest Housing Council. The group sought federal funds to help low-income families move into abandoned and vacant rental units in Park Forest and provided a counseling service to help house hunters understand the cost of residential living (*The Star*, September 22, 1971).

second subsidized housing project—Arbor Trails—would not be entirely subsidized, the excellent planning and construction standards, and the location in the southeast corner of the community kept the project from really becoming an issue in the community. The village was particularly proud of the fact that the buildings occupied only 8 percent of the 52-acre site and that most of the trees were left standing.

The village board supported both racial and economic integration once the issues were raised in the community. It was not the initiator of all decisions, but it worked to facilitate them.

Forest Park.   Although Park Forest was an older community, Forest Park shared many of the characteristics that relate to support for economic integration policies. Both were racially integrated, and the basis of their advertising appeals was the planned nature of the communities, not the exclusiveness. Racial integration in Forest Park occurred gradually, with little, if any, opposition from the residents. While there was a significant black population in the area, Forest Park was one of only a few integrated suburban communities in the north Cincinnati region.[s]

The developer conceived Forest Park as a moderate-income community. Development progressed by "whatever the market would demand." There was no reluctance to get involved with subsidy programs, as the Kanter Corporation got its start through federal Section 608 funding.[t] Residents in the community were concerned about the design and density of dwelling units, but not about cost. There was also little fear of a large influx of blacks from the nearby all-black communities.

The developer became involved in the provision of subsidized housing[u] through default, rather than as part of the planning process.

---

[s]The nearby black communities of Lincoln Heights (lower working class) and Hollydayle (middle class) are described by Harold Rose (1972, pp. 397–432).

[t]Section 608 of the War Housing Insurance Fund, established in 1941, provided funding for one- to four-family units, rental and group housing, and projects of twenty-five or more single family dwellings.

[u]The subsidized single-family subdivision in Forest Park is described below. For more details see Appendix B.

Forest Ridge Subdivision. The area where the approximately 200 units of FHA Section 235 homes are located had been extremely difficult to develop. The site was isolated, set apart from the rest of the community by an Interstate highway. The eastern section of the parcel was purchased in 1968 by a builder who had intended to sell the units under conventional financing. When the builder Imperial Homes, presented the design to the planning commission there was immediate opposition. While the units met all building code requirements, the city felt they would be an eyesore. Residents from the community across the highway also joined in the protest.

The rationale for the decision to convert an original, poorly designed subdivision to FHA Section 235 and encourage other builders to come in under the subsidy program was purely economic. No social objectives were considered.

The city readily approved the building permits for the subsidized single-family homes. The concern of the planning commission and city council was the external design of the original forty-three units. However, there was nothing in their power to prevent construction. There were also no difficulties in approving the plans for the proposed subsidized housing project for the elderly.[v]

Lake Havasu City. As with the decisions relating to economic integration in Park Forest and Forest Park, those in Lake Havasu City were *ad hoc*. The decisions were based on immediate market need.

In 1969 the community had reached a stage of development where there were many workers and few inexpensive places to rent or purchase. In addition, since Lake Havasu City was freestanding, there was no other housing in the vicinity.

Two factors led to the developer's decision to become involved with subsidized housing: (1) immediate need for low-cost housing and (2) an opportunity to experiment. McCulloch had really envisioned some kind of modular or other more innovative techniques. The builder's "innovation" was a type of spray-on stucco.

There were very few participants in the decisions concerning the subsidized housing,[w] only the developer and Shoreline Builders. The FHA office in Phoenix had a minimum amount of contact. At the

---

Despite the very vocal opposition, forty-three units were constructed. Few sold and the builder went bankrupt. The homes then reverted to the Kanter Corporation. It was determined that the only way to salvage the area would be to develop the entire subdivision with homes sold under Section 235. Three other builders constructed a total of 158 homes of more conventional design to complete the subdivision. There were no objections raised to these homes, and all were sold immediately.

[v]This project was called Winton House, Inc. At the times of this study, a plan to build a 120-unit complex for the elderly had been approved by the planning commission, and Winton Forest Church Center, the sponsors, had applied for a mortgage subsidy under FHA Section 236.

[w]Lake Havasu's subsidized subdivision is described below. For more details see Appendix A. *Shoreline.* Robert McCulloch and the President of Shoreline Builders had discussed the possibility of construction of "experimental, innovative" housing in Lake Havasu. Because of the promise of innovative housing and their experience with subsidized housing in the San Francisco Bay area, Shoreline was invited to come into the community. The units which sold for $17,000 to $19,000 were first occupied in spring 1970. Although the sixty-four units have been replete with problems, the developer does not rule out the possibility of future low-cost housing, if it is in line with what the market demands.

time the subdivision was proposed there were no site selection criteria or affirmative marketing requirements.

Unsuccessful Integration Attempts

The history of the unsuccessful attempts at implementing economic and class integration policies in Park Forest South and Irvine demonstrate the importance of strong developer commitment to a marketable integrated community and decisions that contribute to the creation of a community which will accept and continue to support low-cost housing. Various decisions made in both of these communities served to vitiate economic integration objectives.

Village of Park Forest South. Park Forest South received its commitment for a $30 million loan guarantee from HUD in July 1970. Under its project agreement (1971) with the federal government, the developer, Park Forest South Development Company (New Community Enterprises Inc. was subsequently formed to develop the community), was to have provided 500 units of housing for low- and moderate-income families by the end of 1973. However, New Community Enterprises Inc. (NCE), was able to get a delay in meeting the commitment "in order to develop the character of the community first." By the fall of 1973, no subsidized housing existed in Park Forest South. One major abortive attempt had been made,[x] and in Au-

---

[x]The ten-month history of the aborted IHDA-sponsored planned unit development (PUD 1–9) illustrates the dynamics involved in *ad hoc* decisions when all of the participants are not working together from the beginning, when communication is lacking, and when other important manifestations of commitment on the part of the developer are absent.

In early 1972 HUD began to push NCE to build some subsidized housing. Because of the mix criterion of IHDA, NCE approached IHDA, not FHA directly. An application was submitted in the fall of 1972 and the village was informed about the same time.

From the very beginning the proposal was fraught with problems: the plan came as somewhat of a surprise to the planning commission and village board; the site was one of two wooded areas remaining in the community; and, according to one HUD official, "it was a deplorable site plan." After initial approval by the board, plans became stymied when the village held up further approval at the behest of a citizen committee—Save Our Forest Trees (SOFT). SOFT claimed that valuable trees would be destroyed by the construction of the 450-unit complex. SOFT circulated petitions, raised funds, commissioned Governors State University to do a study and contacted local and federal agencies.

In January 1973 SOFT wrote to HUD indicating a desire to "direct our energies toward not only the woods, but also toward the possible acquistion of the land." By March the village planning commission was not certain whether the project should be built. Lewis Manilow claimed he tried to meet his obligations under Title VII. SOFT contended that he was not meeting the environmental statement of the project agreement. SOFT continued its efforts and when three trustee seats were contested during the April election, all candidates went on

gust 1973 a proposal was approved by IHDA to convert forty-six units in a previously unoccupied building under FHA Section 236.[y]

The developer of Park Forest South made the same claim as Jonathan's; that is, subsidized housing would have been built in the community even without the federal guarantee. The veracity of this statement is even more difficult to substantiate. Outside of the project agreement, it is difficult to find formalized plans for economic integration.[z] In addition, the residents of the community were not kept informed about proposals. For example, in January 1973, at a public meeting, Lewis Manilow outlined all projects to be constructed in the community during the coming year. No mention was made of PUD 1–9, which was to include 162 subsidized units (*Park Forest South Post*, January 11, 1973).

NCE's relationship with the planning commission and the village board did not facilitate the approval or implementation of plans. According to a board member, NCE had not kept the city informed about the development of the community and its "surprise attacks" had created much antagonism.

The commitment of the developer must be questioned, given the history of the PUD 1–9 project. The community appeared to share this cynicism. After tracing the history of the demise of the project, a local newspaper article concluded, "Interestingly, NCE Vice-President Kalman Rowen is remembered as having ended several arguments about 1–9 by saying that the woods could easily be saved if someone wanted to buy the land" (*Park Forest South Post*, June 21, 1973). NCE's commitment was attacked somewhat more directly by an official of the Northeast Illinois Planning Commission, "If you

---

record favoring the preservation of the woods. There was little objection at that time to building a smaller project on an unwooded portion of the site. The wooded portion of the site was valued at $525,000. The entire site for PUD 1–9 was about 25 acres. IHDA was willing to finance 200 units in that section of the site as well.

After the election the board was willing to discuss creating a park on the wooded parcels. A resolution to this effect was finally passed. NCE agreed to sell the property and also put up 30 percent matching funds. The village had applied for Bureau of Outdoor Recreation (BOR) funds in February and, if granted, they would account for 50 percent; the federal New Communities Administration was expected to provide the remaining 20 percent. By this action the plans for PUD 1–9 were killed.

[y]*Burnham Oaks*. After PUD 1–9's defeat, NCE converted 46 units in a 59-unit, five-story building to FHA Section 236. The developer had originally wanted to turn the building, which had remained unoccupied since its construction in 1971, into a condominium. See Appendix B for more details.

[z]Mention of an objective of 12 to 15 percent subsidized housing is found in various articles on the community. See for example, Jack Bryan (1972, pp. 282–289).

were a new town developer and really did not want to build low- or moderate-income housing, wouldn't it be good strategy to plan it where you know people would object—that is, in the woods?"

After being "burned," by its own admission, on earlier development proposals, the planning commission refused to hurry along the approval process of PUD 1—9 without careful study. The influence of a citizens' committee on the planning commission and the board, the heightened public interest in the issue, and the coincidental election all contributed to the sounding of the death knell.

The citizens' group, Save Our Forest Trees (SOFT), received a considerable amount of criticism about using ecological issues to block housing for low- and moderate-income families. Leaders of the group did not deny that some may have joined the protest for that reason. However, an effort was made by SOFT to disprove the contention. The organization supported finding another location in the community for a subsidized housing project and made several public disclaimers. It was SOFT's tireless effort that ultimately led to the termination of the plans for PUD 1—9. SOFT believed that NCE was relieved that someone else was being blamed for the failure of the project.[aa]

IHDA cooperated through all stages of the projects' history. In fact, its initial market analysis was too optimistic about the demand for the project (see F.E. Mayo 1972 and Harry Bierman, Jr. 1972).[bb] When it became obvious that the project was in trouble because of the site, IHDA was willing to finance the 200 rental units in another section of the community.

After granting the federal loan guarantee, HUD's next major decision was to allow NCE a delay in implementation of the low- and moderate-income provisions of the project agreement. Two years later, Washington began exerting pressure on the developer to begin to provide the housing. However, HUD did not consult the village on NCE's commitments or obligation. Some communication with the local governmental agencies might have helped resolve the controversy, with some subsidized units being constructed as well.

Irvine. There is no specific mention of providing housing for low- or moderate-income families in the Irvine Plan adopted by Orange County in 1964. The only formal statement concerning economic integration policies came in response to an inquiry from the county's planning office.

[aa]For an alternative interpretation of SOFT's motivations, see Eric Lee Stowe (1974, pp. 114–115).

[bb]A more conservative analysis was done by Susan Goldman (1973).

We recognize that the planning intents thus expressed cannot be fully realized without the provision of housing for people with low incomes. The demand will be there. It will be generated by rising employment levels at Irvine's institutional, commercial and industrial centers, present and future.

The need for a broad spectrum of housing types is inevitable. Attempting to accommodate this need is a prime planning responsibility.

The Irvine Company acknowledges and accepts this responsibility, and subscribes to it as a development requirement.

Accordingly, low-income housing is and will continue to be an element of the Irvine General Plan (Letter to the Orange County Planning Commission from Richard A. Reese, Vice-President—Planning, The Irvine Company, October 30, 1970).

No statement of these goals is made in any of the Irvine advertisements or plans.

The Irvine Company made several aborted attempts at providing moderate-income housing in the community. Prior to incorporation, the county stymied a proposal for a nonsubsidized complex. After incorporation, the City of Irvine killed the same proposal by lowering the density.

In 1970 The Irvine Company went to FHA with a proposal for a 300-unit project to be located on a 15—acre site adjacent to a freeway. FHA rejected the proposal on the grounds that too many units were concentrated on one site and that the noise from the freeway violated environmental noise standards. It suggested that The Irvine Company find another location and scatter the units. Both FHA and The Irvine Company claim that the other was obdurate. Irvine hired consultants to evaluate potential noise problems, but the project never went beyond the initial planning stage.

Prior to incorporation of the community, The Irvine Company submitted a proposal for a 400-acre site with homes to be priced between $25,000 and $27,000. The county planning commission refused to approve the density.

In November 1972, after the city incorporated, the project was revived under the name of Valley View. A series of meetings were held with the city planning commission and residents of the community. Vehement objections were raised to the project and to its potential occupants. At these often hostile meetings, representatives from The Irvine Company attempted to present information which would convince the residents that the units would not be occupied by welfare recipients, that property values would not drop, that the community would not become overrun by minorities and that the schools would not deteriorate.

In February 1973 the planning commission voted to approve the Valley View proposal at a reduced density. The reduction in density raised the estimated costs of the units from $25,000 to $40,000. The residents, still not satisfied, demanded that the entire proposal be defeated. The claim was that moderate-income housing would cause the city to develop an image not intended by the city fathers. One of the city council members added that,

> ... this whole project has been a preconceived attempt to achieve some kind of socioeconomic mix in an area that is not geographically right at this time. . . . And it isn't true that this city is a haven for the rich. We have an exciting melting pot here (Councilman Ray Quigly, quoted in *Irvine World News*, March 9, 1973).

The city planning commission and council did not always vote unanimously against any proposals for low- and moderate-income housing. Two Irvine mayors (Fishback and Pryor) supported a policy of economic integration. In the fall of 1973 Mayor Pryor introduced a proposal aimed at providing new housing for families with a minimum annual income of $11,000. Under the proposal the city would allow slightly higher density. Irvine Pacific, a building subsidiary of The Irvine Company, collaborated on the proposal.

As the above scenario indicates, The Irvine Company attempted on several occasions to provide housing for moderate-income families. These proposals were consistently met with predictable opposition from the residents and local governmental agencies. Since its inception, Irvine was advertised as a high-income, homogeneous community. People were recruited on the premise that Irvine was and would remain a very high status community. No statements concerning balance or openness were included in any marketing efforts.

Because of its marketing practices, The Irvine Company was served with a racial bias suit for failure to comply with the 1968 Civil Rights Act (racial bias in advertising). The implications of marketing practices are evident in a statement made by the former president of The Irvine Company. In response to a question concerning the suit, William R. Mason responded, "The Irvine Company has not made a practice of publicizing its support in the area of fair housing, nor of using our social consciousness as a marketing tool. . . ." (*Los Angeles Times*, April 19, 1973).

FHA officials contended that the Irvine Company had no real intention of following through on the subsidized project. Others in the community expressed the belief, similar to that in Park Forest

South, that the developer was relieved when someone else was to blame for killing a lower-cost housing proposal.

In other communities a sliding scale for land costs facilitated construction of subsidized housing. Although Irvine is being developed on over 50,000 acres and The Irvine Company owned the land for over 100 years, there was no provision for writing down the cost of the land for builders of low-cost housing.

A majority of residents in the community were vehemently opposed to any housing for low- and moderate-income families. They attended any hearings concerning density changes or plans for lower cost housing, and they made their feelings known. They said that they had moved to Irvine to escape the kind of people who would occupy moderate-income housing. Residents were aided by realtors in the community in organized efforts to block any proposals for low- and moderate-income families.

Community Opposition to Economic and Class Integration

The communities of Laguna Niguel, Foster City and North Palm Beach all had to deal with the issue of economic and class integration. In each instance, the proposal for low-cost housing came from outside the community and either the developer, a homeowners' association or a local governmental agency was able to thwart the attempts at integration. In Elk Grove Village, the issue of low-cost housing was raised by a community group, but no positive action was taken by the Village Board of Trustees.

Laguna Niguel. Laguna Niguel had the most detailed plan for economic integration of all the communities in this study. However, representatives of the developer, Avco, made it clear that the following objectives from the plan were not considered seriously,

> ... to help establish adequate housing for all economic levels of the counties (sic) population as site conditions, topography and marketing conditions allow ... to mix housing prices and types as much as possible in every area rather than concentrate neighborhoods of like type and family income level.

> ... those earning less than $6,000 per year will have to live in subsidized housing. It is reasonable to project that about ... 25 percent of the market under $8,600 will be housed in Laguna Niguel and will be disbursed throughout the units (Avco Community Developers Inc. 1971, pp. 11–12).

The one attempt to provide moderate-income housing (nonsubsidized) illustrates the forces that were at work in Laguna Niguel to discourage any attempts at economic and class integration.

In 1969 Kaufman and Broad, one of the largest home builders in the country, purchased a parcel in the community. In 1972 they submitted the plans for a nonsubsidized, 298-unit PUD to the Orange County Planning Commission. Soon after the proposal received approval from the commission, representatives from a homeowners' association went to the county board of supervisors to protest the construction of the units which were to sell for $21,000 to $25,000. Residents had circulated a petition in the community to rally opposition.[cc] The board responded by changing the zoning requirements, which raised the projected cost of the units to a minimum of $30,000. By the middle of 1974 construction had not yet begun.

Foster City. There was no provision for low- or moderate-income housing in the plans of the original developers, the Fosters, or the subsequent owner, Centex West Inc. However, the city was contacted on three occasions by builders with proposals for subsidized housing. All were rejected because of soil problems on one site,[dd] cost restrictions due to the high tax rate and zoning and density requirements.[ee]

The city responded to attempts to provide moderate-income housing by creating more restrictive building requirements. For example, Centex proposed a project with a density of twenty units per acre. The residents wanted ten units per acre; the city council eventually approved seventeen. In 1971 the city applied for federal open space monies, but was turned down because of the lack of low-cost housing.

The residents of Foster City, however, worked to racially integrate the community. At the request of citizens, the Fosters began including minorities in advertisements. In addition, the residents took it upon themselves to place ads in area newspapers drawing attention to the fact that Foster City was a racially integrated community. Foster City had the reputation of being the only open suburban community in the Bay Area. However, this tolerance did not extend to economic and class integration. As indicated above, residents wanted to maintain economic and class homogeneity.

[cc]See Appendix E for the Homeowners' Association objections to the project.

[dd]FHA would not insure homes in various sections of Foster City because of their location on an earthquake fault and land-fill problems.

[ee]The city, for example, required 1200 square feet for a two-bedroom apartment.

North Palm Beach. The city government of North Palm Beach was even more vocal in its opposition to low-cost housing than that of Foster City. The city did not want to get involved with any kind of federal program. In 1971, a church group approached the city with a proposal for a subsidized housing project. There was no possibility that the city would approve it. The city council reacted by upgrading the zoning ordinance.

The community was planned for high- and middle-income families. The dredging of the canals insured the recruitment of high-income, custom-home buyers. North Palm Beach was racially and class segregated, and the city government made certain that it remained so.

Elk Grove Village. The original plan for Elk Grove Village called for a diversity of housing types, but there were no statements concerning low- or moderate-income housing. However, economic and class integration became an issue in 1967, when a shack fire killed two Mexican-American children. The homes were outside the city limits but were within the Village Fire District. When a second fire in 1969 resulted in the death of three more children, the shacks and sheds used as dwellings by migrant workers were bulldozed, after the remaining families had been relocated.

A social action committee of a local church tried to encourage the community to supply housing for the families, and the city held meetings which were heavily attended. The comments made by residents were similar to those made in Irvine during the Valley View controversy. Many residents did not want low-income families living in the community, especially if they were nonwhite. All proposals were defeated and funds were raised to send the families back to their home country.

In 1970 a task force was established to find housing for the families and to survey the community for future housing needs. The task force requested that its status be changed to that of a commission in order to add credibility and authority to the findings. After studying the needs of the 27,000 workers in the Centex Industrial Park, the commission reported, in November 1971, a possible need for 195 to 1055 low- and 172 to 922 moderate-income units in the community for workers in the industrial park, school systems and local government.

In January 1972, the village board of trustees met with the commission, and, according to one commission member, declared that it had no responsibility for Spanish-speaking families and that no other need was indicated for low-income families in the community. In April, the board sent a communication to the housing commission requesting that it undertake an areawide study of housing needs and develop a plan for locating low- and moderate-income housing within the Northwest Cook County area. When the commission continued to focus on the needs of the community, the president of the board of trustees said that he would call for the resignation of the housing commission, *en masse*, if they would not follow the board's policies[ff] (*Elk Grove Herald*, June 25, 1973). After several commission members resigned, the village board waited almost a year before appointing new members. In the interim, the housing commission did not have enough members to constitute a quorum.

Confrontations between the village board and opponents over the issue of low-cost housing continued. In January 1974 the chairman of the planning commission discussed with Centex the possibility of providing some low- or moderate-income housing on a 700-acre site in the community. According to the chairman, William Shannon, Centex did not "appear frightened by the prospect." A member of the board of trustees called for board approval of a resolution directing the planning commission "not to solicit comment on low- or moderate-income housing from builders" (*Elk Grove Herald*, January 24, 1974).

FHA Section 235 and Section 236 programs were too new to be a part of Centex's original plans for the city. However, the developer admitted that there was never any thought given to the provision of low-cost housing of any kind in Elk Grove Village; and Centex perceived that a majority of the residents would vehemently oppose it. Both the village board and village manager felt that the city by itself was not responsible for providing housing for low- or moderate-income families, nor should it be held accountable for the needs of the region. According to one village official, "it is a myth that people should live where they work. If there really were a need, builders would be coming to the city with proposals."

The village fire department was also a very important force in creating an exclusionary policy. It added restrictive codes which, according to a member of the developer's staff, increased the cost of homes while not adding significantly to their safety.

Economic and Class Integration as a "Nonissue"

Economic integration was never an issue in Sharpstown, Valencia or Westlake Village. Sharpstown's developer said that Sharpstown "is not that kind of community," and that there was no need for lower

[ff]The Elk Grove Village Board of Trustees indicated, however, that it would consider moderate-income housing as well as housing for senior citizens in the

cost housing. The developers of Valencia felt "very strongly about not having subsidized housing." The developers of Westlake were more equivocal. On the one hand, they claimed that there was more than an ample supply of low-cost homes in the area. On the other hand, they said that their best selling units in the Village were quad-riminiums selling from $19,000 to $24,000.

Sharpstown. There was never a possibility of low-cost housing being constructed in Sharpstown. Frank Sharp controlled all decisions in the community. Although Sharpstown was within the city limits of Houston, the likelihood of a subsidized housing project being located in the community was very small. A public referendum could have been used to nullify plans for low-income housing.[gg]

Valencia. The Newhall Land and Farming Company planned for a middle-range absorption rate and, until the 1971 earthquake, had succeeded in capturing a good share of the market. The developer felt there was no obligation on the part of private developers to provide subsidized housing, especially because "cash flow problems of new town development conflict with social goals."

Westlake Village. In 1967 John Notter, the President of American-Hawaiian Steamship Company, said that "putting homes for low income families doesn't make sense out here. The investment in land and improvements is such that if we decide to build a $15,000 house—and did it right—we would be able to supply about 900 square feet of space in that housing. No one would buy it" (quoted in Phillip Herrera 1967, p. 67). Five years later the same claims were being made, "Because of significant 'front-end' cost of the Westlake project, housing cannot feasibly be developed for the low income owner" ("Comprehensive Planning of Westlake Village" 1972, p. 3).

The above statements were made publicly. Privately, there was some concern about the viability of marketing a community so top-heavy with high-priced homes. The least expensive single-family detached homes in Westlake sold for $45,000 to $50,000. The new City of Thousand Oaks' Plan required a minimum of 64 percent single-family homes, 16 percent attached single-family, and 20 percent cluster housing. And most development during the next ten years would take place on the 4700 acres located in Thousand Oaks.

---

village if private developers would make land available for such housing and if it would essentially comply with the village's zoning and building codes.

[gg]Filomeno Rodriquez, Jr. (1973) has explored the low-cost housing problem in Houston.

While economic integration was not an issue in Westlake Village, the developers were involved in a racial bias suit which was the culmination of a four-year effort to have Westlake's advertising comply with Section 804(c) of the 1968 Civil Rights' Act. An out-of-court settlement was reached in August 1973, when the developers agreed to use minority models in all advertisements and to undertake a "special creative advertising program to attract customers from minority groups" (San Fernando Valley Fair Housing Council Newsletter, August 1973).

Summary: Policies and Strategies
for Economic and Class Integration

Statements about new communities providing a wide range of housing opportunities for persons of all income levels pervade the new community literature, plans and some advertisements. For example, of all the communities in the study, Laguna Niguel had the most elaborate scheme for the allocation of low- and moderate-income housing as part of its comprehensive plan (Avco Community Developers Inc. 1971). However, there was no relation between that plan and what existed in the community. As the information presented above indicates, commitment to developing an economically balanced community goes beyond the conception of the type of community planned or statements in the general plan. Three of the communities—Columbia, Reston and Jonathan—had developers who followed through with decisions that indicate a commitment to providing housing for persons priced out of the traditional housing market. The developers of Park Forest South and Irvine both indicated support of the goal of economic integration, the former through involvement in the federal new communities program. However, the behavior of both of these developers did not facilitate attainment of that goal.

Park Forest, Forest Park and Lake Havasu City never had stated economic integration policy objectives. However, related developer decisions and policies created a nonexclusionary ethos and the communities all accepted subsidized housing. The issue of low-cost housing was raised in Elk Grove Village, Foster City and Laguna Niguel. In each of these communities either the developer or the local governmental agency opposed any involvement.

The older communities of Sharpstown and North Palm Beach and the newer California communities of Westlake Village and Valencia planned to be residentially homogeneous and remained so. The provision of subsidized housing in these new communities was a "nonissue."

WHAT ACCOUNTS FOR ECONOMIC AND CLASS INTEGRATION?

A "New Breed" of Developer and Perception of the Market

While new community developers may view themselves as a "new breed," building cities, not subdivisions, they are all driven by the profit motive.

> As a rule, then, few communities intend to offer houses at less than $20,000 during their first few years of marketing. This figure is not set entirely by costs or by the high land prices paid by merchant builders who construct the houses in new communities. It is the result of a conscious desire by community builders to create for their developments a certain kind of image, based on their perceptions of market behavior and future values (Eichler and Kaplan 1970, p. 50).

These market decisions to create entire cities for the middle and upper classes raise serious questions concerning the public interest. The issue is raised not only because a large segment of the population is excluded from the new community market, but also because of the impact on surrounding areas. In Orange County, California, Irvine is only one of many new communities in the area, none with housing for low- or moderate-income families. The city of Santa Ana, where a majority of the county's poor and nonwhite live, is concerned over the economic balkanization of the region.[hh]

Most of the developers privately subscribed to the contention that new communities offer enough other desirable marketing appeals that low-cost housing ("if done correctly") would not seriously damage the market. For example, while the developer of Westlake Village felt that there was no need for low-cost housing in the community and did not want to see it there, he did concede that it would, in no way, hurt the housing market.

The reality is that most developers respond to market demand, not need. In 1972 the largest housing market consultants on the West Coast had 500 requests for analyses of areas of California. None of these requests concerned low-cost housing. Personal value judgements

[hh]In 1970 Santa Ana hired consultants to determine the effects of the incorporation of Irvine on the area. Their report concluded that the key issue involved is the public interest. The primary questions to be answered include: what "publics" are involved—the residents of the new community, the county, the state? How should decisions be made about what is in the public interest—unilaterally by the developer or by public approval? See Barton-Aschman Associates, Inc. (1970, p. 6).

usually overrode market needs. The developers of Columbia, Reston and Jonathan anticipated market need as well as demand. In the case of Lake Havasu City, subsidized housing was the response to immediate demand. Forest Park's and Park Forest's decisions were also *ad hoc*. A determination was made that subsidized housing would maximize return on the sites at that time. This also was a factor in Jonathan, which was not located in a "seller's market."

The consequences of developer decisions on the housing market are examined in Chapter 7.

Demographics of Area

As indicated in Chapter 2, no suburban area has its share of low-income families. For example, it has been estimated that over 40 percent of the annual housing demand in the Minneapolis–St. Paul area reflects the needs of low- and moderate-income families. The greatest concentration of these families is in the central city area with a few in the northern suburbs. Suburbanization in the area has been an almost exclusively high-income phenomenon and a widely dispersed one. The needs of moderate-income families which Jonathan met were primarily those of families from rural areas.

One factor that has, most likely, facilitated the acceptance of subsidized housing in the suburban areas is the very small percentage of minorities in the Minneapolis–St. Paul area. Minorities comprised only 2.3 percent of the population; three-quarters of that percentage was black, the remainder Native American, Chicano and Asian. And about 5 percent of the black population lived in suburban locations.

However, the high percentage of minorities in the Baltimore and Washington areas did not effect the acceptance of low-income families in Columbia and Reston. The developer's marketing strategy had a greater impact.

Resident Recruitment

As was documented, the developer's marketing strategy has significant impact on resident acceptance of housing for low-income families. For example, Columbia residents, through the Columbia Association, worked to see that Columbia reached its 10 percent objective. A task force was created to assess needs and make proposals.[ii] Members of the task force worked hard to provide citizen input into the planning process. Rouse created expectations for

[ii]See for example, "Report to the Columbia Task Force on a 'Balanced Community' and the Commitment to 10% Subsidized Housing in Columbia, Maryland" (1971; and Columbia Association, Office of Planning and Evaluation (1974).

socioeconomic integration which they wanted to see met. They were constantly reminding the developer of his goals and they utilized the local newspapers as a sounding board for their proposals. These residents did not create the "favorable climate." The developer's early actions and policies, particularly the marketing strategy, led to the recruitment of residents who supported the goal of socioeconomic integration. If Rouse had not made his objectives clear or had delayed in their implementation, he may have met with a negative response on the part of the residents.

Members of the Housing Committee of the Reston Community Association also felt that they had had a tremendous influence on Gulf-Reston Inc. The tendency, without their input, would have been to address the needs of the upper-income residents only and to ignore the needs of those priced out of the private housing market. Simon had sold these early "pioneer" residents on the idea of low- and moderate-income housing.

Geography and Political Climate

It is frequently claimed that one of the reasons that Columbia was able to institute a policy of socioeconomic integration was the sympathetic political and social climate of the area. Unfortunately, this was not the case.[jj] The subsidized housing project sponsored by the Interfaith group in Columbia was the first in Howard County and the first to be processed by the Baltimore Regional FHA office. Although the county planning board had documented the need for lower-cost housing, the county commissioners were not enthusiastic over the proposal. However, in order to receive federal water and sewer funds, a workable program was needed. This did not guarantee full county cooperation. Political pressure was needed to get the program through HUD, and once funding was obtained, there was only half-hearted cooperation. There were delays in connecting water and electricity lines. The county also wanted prepayment on water and sewer taps. Although Maryland law had a provision that allowed assisted housing to make less than full tax payments, the county collected the full amount on the Interfaith project.

Primarily because of the attitudes and actions of the Columbia residents, much of the county's original hostile stance changed. The county became much more responsive to the needs of low-income families and, led by Columbia residents, the county formed a housing

---

[jj]The attitudes and opinions of the residents and developer of Columbia often stand in sharp contrast with the rest of the county. For example in 1964 Howard County voted for Wallace. In 1968 Nixon carried Howard County by a substantial margin, but was defeated in Columbia by better than 2–1.

committee. More important, the county sponsored a subsidized housing project.

Despite evidence to the contrary, developers cite region as a factor in facilitation of integration policies. Raymond Watson, President of The Irvine Company, was quoted as saying, "In Columbia, they ran full page ads showing inter-racial couples. Back there, that went over great. But if I tried it here, I'd scare off every white persons I had even the slightest hope of getting."[kk]

In order to test the region hypothesis more systematically, the same questions concerning socioeconomic integration were asked in conventional communities, matched on demographic characteristics and located in close proximity to the sample new communities. The results offer some discrediting evidence for the region theory. Significantly more of the respondents in the conventional communities paired with the class-integrated communities were opposed to housing for low- and moderate-income families. For example, over 58 percent of the respondents in the conventional community paired with Jonathan objected to housing selling for less than $25,000 in their neighborhood; 65 percent in Columbia's paired conventional community, 62 percent in Park Forest's, 51 percent in Forest Park's and 47 percent in Reston's.[ll] However, residents in the California communities displayed even greater opposition.

Government Intervention

Government intervention to encourage communities to provide housing for low- and moderate-income families can take several forms. For example, one of the unanticipated consequences of a Simon decision was more subsidized housing in Reston. Simon had made an agreement with former secretary of the Interior, Stuart Udall, for the relocation of the United States Geological Survey Headquarters in Reston. Just before the contract was to be signed, the Washington Metropolitan Housing Authority and the Housing Opportunities Council brought a class-action suit against the General Services Administration and Gulf-Reston for noncompliance with Executive Order No. 11512. Eligibility criteria for sites under this order include an "adequate available supply of decent and non-segre-

[kk]Quoted by David Shaw (1970). This claim has been disputed by many. Shaw notes that Howard County, where Columbia is located, is "every bit as conservative and even more rural than Orange County" (Irvine's location), and that the developer "met hostile, organized resistance before gaining the confidence and cooperation of county officials" (p. 196).

[ll]In Jonathan housing selling for less than $25,000 was objected to by 12 percent of the residents, in Columbia 23 percent; in Park Forest 37 percent; in Forest Park, 37 percent; and 37 percent in Reston.

gated housing with Area of Expected Residency within price range of agency's employees" (Carol Whittaker Rende 1971, p. 14). The suit resulted in an agreement by Gulf-Reston to provide 688 more subsidized housing units in the community and 1300 other low-cost (nonsubsidized) units.

The result of a government facility locating in Reston was the construction of close to 2000 low-cost units in the community. This was not the outcome of the government's acquistion of the one-million-square-foot Rockwell International facility in Laguna Niguel.

Before the federal government could acquire the facility, the General Services Administration (GSA) had to file a statement on the adequacy of housing for the projected 1000 to 1500 employees. An analysis done by HUD concluded that "a commuting distance of more than ten miles would impose a severe and unnecessary hardship for low- and moderate-income families" (General Services Administration 1973, p. 17). GSA, "on the basis of normally accepted commuting customs in Orange County," requested that HUD do another study widening the area to 15 or 20 miles from the site. GSA officials felt that "a 20 to 25 mile radius is more realistic since a daily commute distance by workers in this area of California is customary" (General Services Administration 1973). This 20−mile radius extends to the city of Santa Ana where a majority of the low- and moderate-income housing in the area is located. Without any commitment for low- and moderate-income housing from the developer, GSA approved the acquisition of the site in March 1974. If the Orange County Fair Housing Council or some other group had brought suit against GSA, as was done in Reston, some low-cost housing might have resulted.[mm]

Another government intervention device is the fair share plan. As mentioned in Chapter 2 several areas of the country are adopting this strategy. In January 1972 the Metropolitan Council of the Twin Cities Area (Minneapolis−St. Paul) adopted a housing allocation plan which assigned municipalities to one of four priority areas depending

---

[mm]Government agency relocation is causing controversy over racial as well as low-cost housing issues. For example, "several years ago, the U.S. Postal Service announced it was going to build twenty-one new bulk-mail centers and twelve auxiliary service facilities around the country. Most of the thirty-three sites are in new suburban areas, sparking criticism that the new system is part of a growing practice within the federal government to shift its operations away from the central core cities—resulting in reducing the number of black and minority group workers. Federal spokesmen deny that there are any racial considerations in such moves. They argue that the cost of operations in the city has gone up tremendously and that the availability of space outside the central core, and the movement of large numbers of workers to the suburbs have made suburban sites more attractive" (Francis Ward 1975).

on the availability of various services and facilities (Metropolitan Council of the Twin Cities Area 1973a). The Council had A−95 review power for water and sewer funds and used it to encourage the provision of subsidized housing in the suburbs.[nn] If Jonathan did not already have subsidized housing, it would have theoretically been required to provide some under the plan. If it were an ordinary subdivision, it would have an area priority of "2." However, since it had the facilities and services of a city, it received a rating of "1."[oo]

Fairfax County took several actions which enhanced the goal of increasing the supply of low- and moderate-income housing. It allowed builders to take various short cuts in construction, substituting aluminum siding and plastic pipes for more expensive materials and narrowing street requirements. It was still impossible to bring in a new home for less than $27,000. The board of supervisors in 1971 passed an ordinance requiring each subdivision to provide 6 percent low- and 9 percent moderate-income housing. Except for Planned Community Zoning, every aspect of the ordinance was challenged in court on the basis of state law forbidding covenants in zoning. The ordinance was revised so that the county could work on all requests for rezoning to encourage some low- and moderate-income housing.

The county also created a fund to assist developers with the cost of water and sewer taps. Two of the projects in Reston received some of this money, and funds had been allocated to Tall Oaks.

Not all new community-local government relations were so helpful in facilitating integration. The Orange County Board of Supervisors, for example, had a record of being unsympathetic to the needs of the poor, especially in the area of housing. It failed to provide the leadership necessary to inspire commitment on the part of communities in the county. It was only after heated debate that the board adopted a housing element in October 1971. However, the element was aimed primarily at upgrading substandard housing and was applicable only to unincorporated areas.

At the time of the incorporation of the City of Irvine, the state local agency formation commission was the only agency that had power to require some kind of commitment to low-income housing. It failed to meet its mandated responsibility.

[nn]In 1972 the metropolitan area's total supply of subsidized housing increased 22 percent over the 1970−71 period. Of the almost 30,000 units approved or proposed, 76 percent were located in Minneapolis or St. Paul. The suburban share doubled from the previous year, from 12 to 24 percent. A total of sixty-three communities had taken initiatives in subsidized housing as of July 1972 and twenty-two communities and one county had created Housing and Redevelopment Authorities. Metropolitan Council of the Twin Cities (1973b).

[oo]See Appendix F for a map of the priority areas.

With the key exception of one member, the city council was firmly opposed to involvement with any housing proposals which included federal subsidies. The city council also voted to defeat a plan for densities needed for a large moderate-income project.

The planning commission voted (four-to-three) to include the requirement that a new village planned for 27,000 people include 5 to 10 percent moderate-income housing (homes selling for $27,000).

Jonathan was in a somewhat unique position. It was annexed by an existing community and is now within the jurisdictional boundaries of the city of Chaska. Soon after Jonathan received its federal loan guarantee, the developer came to the city with proposals for FHA Section 235 and Section 236 housing. No real problems or negative reaction was encountered. The proposals got through the planning commission, public hearings and the city council without any complaints. The smooth working relationship was partially a result of the fact that the president of the Jonathan Development Corporation was a native of Chaska and the former City Attorney. There was later some concern that the city of Chaska was becoming hesitant to approve additional subsidized projects because of the tax differential for subsidized projects under existing state law. This tax differential was part of the reason Jonathan was trying to develop alternative methods of financing lower cost housing.

Looking at the record of other new communities participating under the 1970 federal new communities legislation does not provide any evidence to support the contention that the federal government is helping to fill a void created by strictly private development (see Table 3—1). The provision of housing for low- and moderate-income families appears to be concomitant with the generally slow development and financial difficulties of the federally assisted new communities. Given the inchoate status of the new communities program and the problems in staffing and administrative support,[pp] a wholesale indictment of the federal involvement is inappropriate. However, in the case of Park Forest South, it is the commitment of the developer which must be questioned.

The developer of Jonathan maintained that housing to match the needs of residents in the metropolitan area would have been built whether Jonathan had received a federal loan guarantee or not and

[pp]For a description of the early problems faced by the New Communities Administration see, U.S. Congress, House Committee on Banking and Currency (1973), especially the testimony of former Director William Nicoson. For an analyses of the administration and implementation of the New Communities Act see Rabinovitz and Smookler, (1973) and Smookler (1975).

that Henry McKnight was dedicated to the policy of socioeconomic integration. However, in the initial proposal to HUD, plans were not operationalized toward that objective. Hence, it is difficult to speculate as to the credibility of the claim.

The major government incentive program for economic and class integration of suburbs is the federal new communities program. It is difficult to determine the influencing role of involvement with the federal new communities program in Jonathan's integration policies. It is safe to assume, however, that there was not a straight casual relationship between participation in the federal program and provision of subsidized housing. All of the other factors described earlier in the chapter had a strong, if not overwhelming, effect. There is some question, however, as to whether the community itself would have been built without a federal loan guarantee.

The consequences of these policy decisions and strategies for integration are evaluated in Chapter 7. The correlates of resident support for integration and the importance of the location of subsidized units are discussed in the next chapter.

Chapter 6

Correlates of Integration: Resident Attitudes

Among the key factors that affect the feasibility and stability of integration are the levels of tolerance and prejudice.[a] The assumption, as discussed in Chapter 2, is that a majority of people would rather live in homogeneous environments. If the veracity of the contentions concerning preferences for homogeneity and status are accepted, then several disparate conclusions might be drawn about the people who live in integrated communities. One simple explanation is that they are not like most people; that is, they differ in demographic characteristics. However, as discussed in Chapter 4, they are very similar to residents in the segregated communities. Other possible interpretations might be that they may have chosen to live where they do out of necessity and still desire to live in a homogeneous environment or that the high quality of amenities in the new communities may have helped sway the middle- and higher-income residents to accept some degree of social integration. These theories are tested in this chapter.

PERCEPTION OF COMMUNITY

The data presented in the next chapter show that the residents of the integrated communities do perceive the diversity in their community. When asked if the "people who live in the community are pretty much the same," only 55 percent agreed, compared to 70 percent in the homogeneous communities. However, residents in both types

[a]See Hawley and Rock (1973) for a review of factors involved in racial and economic integration.

of communities evaluated other residents very similarly. When asked if they saw the type of people in the community as "better" than in their previous place of residence, 48 percent of the respondents in the integrated and 46 percent in the segregated communities responded affirmatively (figures do not include residents of subsidized housing; see Table 7–1).

If class image is so important to the purchase decision, greater acceptance of the lower status residents may have occurred after moving to a community. However, both sets of respondents reported approximately the same effect of the move to their respective communities on their quality of life. Sixty-seven percent of those in the segregated and 65 percent of those in the integrated communities said that there had been improvement. Seventy-seven percent of the respondents living in the integrated communities and 81 percent of those living in the segregated communities said that they would advise friends or relatives to move to their respective communities.

ECONOMIC AND CLASS INTEGRATION

Given the low economic status of many blacks, racial and economic discrimination factors are difficult to separate. There are many, though, who contend that with the rising income of blacks and changing patterns of white attitudes, racial integration is becoming much more facile.[b]

Unfortunately, this appears to be speculation at the moment. Although the attitudes of white Americans toward interracial neighborhoods have become increasingly more favorable,[c] the country's housing has become more segregated. The Taeubers, analyzing the interrelation between racial and socioeconomic residential segregation, concluded that,

> ... residential segregation is a more tenacious social problem than economic discrimination. Improving the economic status of Negroes is unlikely by itself to alter prevailing patterns of racial segregation (Karl E. Taeuber and Alma F. Taeuber 1965, p. 95).

[b]Downs (1973b, p. 10) has stated that he believes that the middle class desire for racial dominance will gradually disappear in the minds of many (but not all) white Americans. This will occur as more and more whites discover that minority group individuals with the same incomes as their own share the same values and behavior patterns.

[c]In a study of metropolitan Detroit, for example, Otis Dudley Duncan, Howard Schuman and Beverly Duncan (1973, p. 99) found a significant drop over a thirteen-year period in the percentage of people who would be unhappy or disturbed if blacks of the same income and education level moved into the neighborhoods (54 to 28 percent). See also, Angus Campbell (1971) and Norman Bradburn Seymour Sudman and Galen L. Gockel (1971).

The findings of this study provide some credibility for the assertion that it is becoming easier to integrate racially than by class. For all of the respondents in the sample, opposition to housing for low- and moderate-income families vaired according to the race and life cycle of these families. For example, there was less resistance to housing for retired persons earning less than $5000 annually than for other families in that income category (Figure 6−1).[d] While opposition to blacks decreased as their income went up, it was still greater than opposition to whites in all income and life-cycle categories (Figure 6−2). Seventy-nine percent of the residents said housing for families earning less than $5000 per year would harm their neighborhood, and 14 percent responded similarly for blacks earning more than $15,000. Although opposition to racial integration was small at the upper income levels, resistance to blacks as opposed to whites increased with the income level of the target groups. Opposition to blacks with incomes of less than $5000 annually was only 1.1 times greater than to whites in the same category (79 percent vs. 74 per-

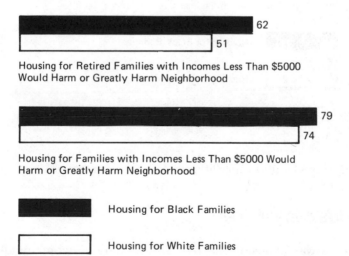

Percent of Respondents Who Felt That Housing For Low-Income Black and White Families Would Harm or Greatly Harm Neighborhood

62
51

Housing for Retired Families with Incomes Less Than $5000 Would Harm or Greatly Harm Neighborhood

79
74

Housing for Families with Incomes Less Than $5000 Would Harm or Greatly Harm Neighborhood

Housing for Black Families

Housing for White Families

Figure 6−1. Resident Opposition to Housing for Low-Income Black and White Families

[d]See Appendix G for attitudes toward racial and class integration in each community.

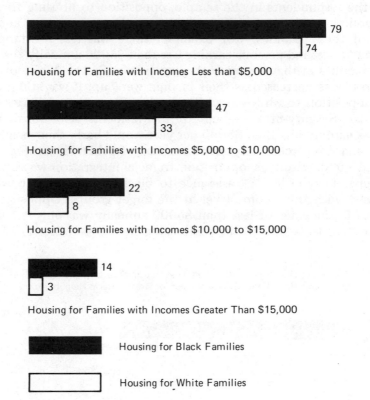

Percent of Respondents Who Felt That Housing For Each Family
Type Would Harm or Greatly Harm Neighborhood

79
74

Housing for Families with Incomes Less than $5,000

47
33

Housing for Families with Incomes $5,000 to $10,000

22
8

Housing for Families with Incomes $10,000 to $15,000

14
3

Housing for Families with Incomes Greater Than $15,000

Housing for Black Families

Housing for White Families

Figure 6–2. Resident Opposition to Housing for Income and Racial Groups

cent); at the $15,000 range it was 4.7 times greater (14 percent vs. 3 percent).[e]

ATTITUDE CORRELATES

Attitudes toward housing for low- and moderate-income families for the entire sample (N = 2891) are presented in Figures 6–1 and 6–2.[f] The key variables which consistently accounted for variance in these

[e]See Appendix H for the effect of the question sequence on responses to the neighborhood mix items.

[f]None of the class or race integration attitudes includes the responses of residents who were living in subsidized housing.

attitudes include: the existence of subsidized housing in the community; the value of the respondent's dwelling unit; whether the respondent owned or rented; and a contextual variable that measures concern for status.[g]

Class Integration—Existence of Subsidized Housing

Figure 6-3 shows the impact of the existence of subsidized housing on attitudes toward neighborhood economic integration. On each of the measures, residents in the integrated communities were considerably less hostile toward integration than those in homogeneous communities. This effect is demonstrated dramatically for each community in Figure 6-4.[h]

Given the demographic similarity between the residents of homogeneous and integrated communities and the differences in attitudes toward economic integration, some amount of self-selection or attitude change after moving to the communities must have been occurring.

There has been considerable research on attitude change through interracial contact. It has been found that racial prejudice is reduced through contact; and that behavior change typically precedes rather than follows from attitude change.[i] In addition, physical proximity has been shown to act as a catalyst for the attitude change.[j] However, most of the conclusions have been based on research of contact between persons of equal status.

The findings of this study provide evidence that attitude change can occur through contact with persons of different status, and proximity has considerable effect (see Table 6-1). Respondents who lived closest to subsidized housing were significantly less likely to object to racial and economic integration. Persons who lived more

[g]See Appendix I for a listing of items included in the index.

[h]Park Forest South's announcement of conversion of forty-six units to FHA Section 236 was made subsequent to the household survey.

[i]Interviews with housewives in two housing projects—one integrated, one segregated—showed that the integrated pattern reduced prejudice. Tenants in the integrated projects were no less prejudiced initially than those in the segregated projects. See Morton Deutsch and Mary Collins (1951).

[j]In a follow-up study to Deutsch and Collins it was found that persons living near blacks were more likely than those living further away to report contact, "to anticipate that white friends in the project would approve of such contact, and to have high esteem for the Negroes in the project, to approve of the biracial aspect of the Project, and to have a favorable attitude toward Negroes in general" (Daniel M. Wilner, Rosabelle P. Walkely and S.W. Cook 1955, p. 6). Also see George Simpson and Milton J. Yinger (1973), and Thomas F. Pettigrew (1973) for reviews of contact hypothesis literature.

Percent of Respondents in Each Type of Community

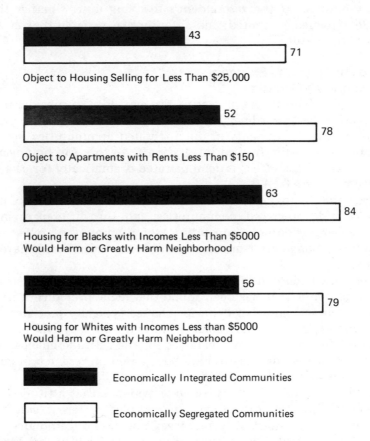

Object to Housing Selling for Less Than $25,000

43

71

Object to Apartments with Rents Less Than $150

52

78

Housing for Blacks with Incomes Less Than $5000
Would Harm or Greatly Harm Neighborhood

63

84

Housing for Whites with Incomes Less than $5000
Would Harm or Greatly Harm Neighborhood

56

79

Economically Integrated Communities

Economically Segregated Communities

Figure 6–3.   Attitudes toward Neighborhood Socioeconomic
Integration by Community Differentiation

than a half-mile from the subsidized housing were still considerably
less likely to oppose integration than those living in the segregated
communities.

The effect of self-selection is difficult to determine, but several
tests were made. Residents were asked what factors were important
in their dwelling unit choice. The percentage mentioning "type of
people in neighborhood" was insignificant. One indication from the
household survey data that self-selection is a factor, is that persons
who moved into communities after subsidized housing had been
built were significantly more likely to approve of housing for low-
and moderate-income families than those who lived there prior to
its existence. However, this variable did not account for much of

Percent of Respondents Who Objected to Housing Selling
for Less Than $25,000

Community	Percent
Jonathan	12
Columbia	23
Park Forest	37
Forest Park	37
Reston	37
Park Forest South	43
Lake Havasu City	48
Sharpstown	52
North Palm Beach	61
Elk Grove Village	61
Irvine	62
Valencia	65
Foster City	67
Westlake Village	72
Laguna Niguel	78

■ Economically Integrated Communities

□ Economically Segregated Communities

Figure 6–4. Preference for Neighborhood Residential Homogeneity by New Community

Table 6–1. Relationship of Community Residential Differentiation to Attitudes Toward Socioeconomic Integration[a]
(percent of respondents by community differentiation categories)

Attitude toward Integration	Distance to Nearest Subsidized Housing		No Subsidized Housing	Chi Square Significance Level	Gamma
	< 1/2 mile	> 1/2 mile			
Object to housing selling for less than $25,000 in neighborhood	23	38	63	.001	.52
Object to dwelling units renting for less than $150 in neighborhood	24	49	69	.001	.49
Housing for blacks with incomes less than $5000 would harm or greatly harm neighborhood	38	74	84	.001	.46
Housing for whites with incomes less than $5000 would harm or greatly harm neighborhood	35	66	79	.001	.44
Sample size	306	850	1,731		

[a]Figures do not include responses of persons living in subsidized housing.

the variance in attitudes when it was utilized in multiple regression analyses.

In each of the communities with subsidized housing, no effort was made to hide the fact from prospective residents. Columbia, Jonathan and Reston included this information in their sales brochures. This knowledge obviously had a synergetic impact on selection.

Status Concern

Simple snobbery or status concern correlated very highly with opposition to economic and racial integration (Table 6–2). This variable accounted for much of the variation within communities and appears to distinguish between respondents in the segregated and integrated communities. There were more "high status concern" persons in the homogeneous communities. Again, because of the demographic similarities of both groups of residents, it is difficult to specify how much self-selection or attitude change accounts for the variation in this index.

Dwelling Unit Value

Opposition to housing for low- and moderate-income families was positively correlated with the value of the respondent's dwelling unit. For all respondents opposition to multifamily units was greater than for single-family.[k] Attitudes toward low-cost single-family housing by respondents' dwelling unit value are shown in Figure 6–5.

Owners and Renters

Renters were significantly more favorable toward class integration than homeowners. This conforms to findings of other studies on racial integration.[l] Many explanations have been given for this correlation. Renters do not have to be as concerned about property values, since they do not have a financial stake in their dwelling unit, and renters tend to be younger. The young are less fearful of the impact of integration.[m] However, as will be shown below, age ac-

[k]"The St. Louis County Planning Department recently estimated the relative costs and revenues produced by developing a 132-apartment complex or single-family dwellings on the same 13-acre site. The agency found that building the apartment complex would result in a net surplus of revenue over service costs. Building single-family homes would result in a net loss" (Daniel Lauber 1973, p. 2).

[l]In contrast to the results of most studies, Deborah Hensler found "among suburbanites controlling for class, renters are as much as 15 percent more likely to favor segregation as compared to homeowners" (Frederick M. Wirt, Benjamin Walter, Francine F. Rabinovitz and Deborah R. Hensler 1972, p. 112).

[m]Gruen and Gruen (1972, p. 53) also found those under forty-five years old much more positive toward economic mix.

Table 6–2.   Relationship between Residents' Status Concern and Attitudes Toward Neighborhood Socioeconomic and Racial Integration[a] *(percent of respondents in each status concern level)*

Integration Attitudes	Status Concern					Chi Square Significance Level	Gamma
	Low → High						
	Low				High		
Object to housing selling for <$25,000 in neighborhood	46	50	61	62	66	.001	.21
Prefer persons of same educational level in neighborhood	23	29	37	34	42	.001	.18
Prefer persons of same race in neighborhood	11	20	24	23	35	.001	.24
Housing for blacks with incomes <$5000 would harm or greatly harm neighborhood	65	76	85	82	87	.001	.27
Housing for whites with incomes <$5000 would harm or greatly harm neighborhood	62	70	79	78	81	.001	.21
Negative reaction to blacks moving into neighborhood	7	15	28	23	30	.001	.24
Sample size	476	831	483	452	498		

[a]Figures do not include responses of persons living in subsidized housing.

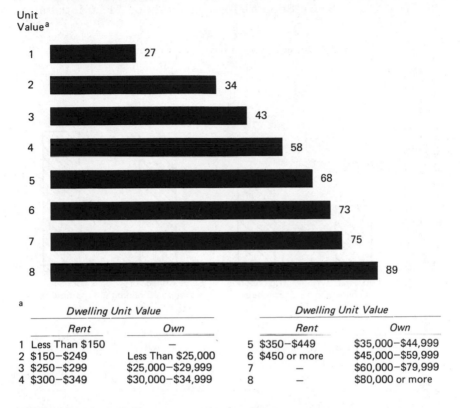

Percent of Respondents Who Objected to Housing Selling
for Less Than $25,000

Unit Value[a]		
1		27
2		34
3		43
4		58
5		68
6		73
7		75
8		89

[a]

	Dwelling Unit Value				Dwelling Unit Value	
	Rent	Own			Rent	Own
1	Less Than $150	—	5	$350–$449		$35,000–$44,999
2	$150–$249	Less Than $25,000	6	$450 or more		$45,000–$59,999
3	$250–$299	$25,000–$29,999	7	—		$60,000–$79,999
4	$300–$349	$30,000–$34,999	8	—		$80,000 or more

Figure 6—5. Preference for Neighborhood Residential
Homogeneity by Respondents' Dwelling Unit Value

counted for some variance in racial attitudes, but for very little in
economic and class integration attitudes.

Individual Attributes

Income, age, race and occupation do not account for as much of
the variance in economic and class integration attitudes as the variables listed above. As expected, higher income persons were more
opposed to mix. However, partially due to double incomes in many
families and recent trends in wage categories, income did not consistently explain variation in attitudes.[n]

[n]Angus Campbell (1971, p. 51) reached the same conclusion about income
and occupation as predictors of racial attitudes.

While education correlated with both attitudes toward economic and racial integration, the direction of the relationship was not the same (see Figure 6–6). Support for neighborhood racial integration

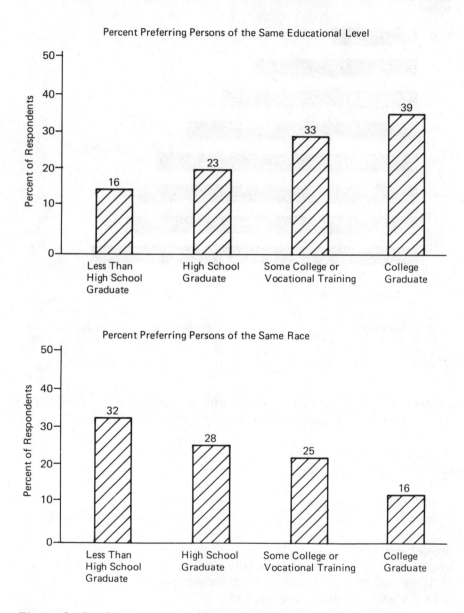

Figure 6–6.   Preference for Neighborhood Class Homogeneity and Racial Segregation by Educational Level of Respondent

increased with the educational level of the respondent, but for economic integration support decreased.

Black respondents were consistently more favorable toward socioeconomic balance. However, the pattern of responses paralleled that of whites. For example, 71 percent of whites and 50 percent of blacks felt that housing for whites earning less than $5000 would harm their neighborhood; 77 percent of white and 53 percent of black respondents gave a similar response for black families earning less than $5000.

Summary of Attitude Correlates

Table 6—3 presents the results of multiple regression analyses of predictors of attitudes toward socioeconomic integration. For each of the measures the community differentiation variable—existence of subsidized housing—accounted for a significant proportion of the variance. Residents in integrated communities, especially those who lived in close proximity to subsidized housing, were most likely to support economic integration. Low status concern also correlated highly with positive integration attitudes. The two dwelling-unit characteristics, high value and ownership, related strongly to opposition to economic mix. Individual attributes—age, race, income and occupation—while significant on some of the measures did not account for much of the variance.

The importance of community residential and racial characteristics is demonstrated again in Table 6—4. When the variable of racial integration was substituted into the equations, it also accounted for a significant amount of the variance.

Table 6–3. Multiple Regression Analysis: Attitudes Toward Neighborhood Socioeconomic Integration

Dependent and Predictor Variables	Simple Correlation Coefficient	Beta Coefficient	F Ratio	Cumulative R^2
Objection to Housing Selling for Less Than $25,000				
Predictors				
Dwelling unit value	-.33	-.30	283.9	.11
Subsidized housing in community	-.25	-.18	98.9	.14
Status concern	-.16	-.17	91.2	.17
N = 2743				
Housing for Blacks with Incomes Less Than $5000 Will Harm or Greatly Harm Neighborhood				
Predictors				
Subsidized housing in community	.21	.16	73.5	.04
Status concern	.19	.18	92.3	.08
Own-rent	-.18	-.13	42.8	.10
Race	-.12	-.11	36.7	.12
Income	.14	.11	29.8	.13
Age	.16	.07	14.0	.13
Education	-.07	-.05	6.3	.13
Occupation	.02	.04	3.7	.14
N = 2542				

Housing for Whites with Incomes
Less Than $5000 Will Harm or Greatly
Harm Neighborhood

Predictors				
Subsidized housing in community	.20	.16	75.4	.04
Own-rent	-.18	-.14	52.2	.07
Status concern	.14	.14	57.5	.09
Income	.17	.12	39.1	.10
Race	-.10	-.09	24.7	.11

N = 2550

Table 6–4. Multiple Regression Analysis: Attitudes Toward Neighborhood Racial Integration

Dependent and Predictor Variables	Simple Correlation Coefficient	Beta Coefficient	F Ratio	Cumulative R^2
Prefer Persons of Same Race in Neighborhood				
Predictors				
Status concern	.21	.18	99.7	.04
Community racially integrated	.19	.15	65.5	.07
Age	.21	.12	43.0	.10
Education	-.15	-.10	28.1	.11
Race	-.11	-.09	23.2	.12
Own-rent	-.09	-.06	9.2	.12
N = 2725				
Positive Reaction to Blacks Moving Into Neighborhood				
Predictors				
Status concern	-.18	-.16	68.8	.03
Age	-.17	-.12	38.0	.06
Education	.10	.05	7.8	.06
Community racially integrated	-.09	-.06	9.1	.06
Own-rent	.08	.07	9.0	.06
Dwelling unit value	-.02	.04	2.1	.07
N = 2645				

Chapter 7

Consequences of Integration

ECONOMIC AND CLASS INTEGRATION: THE LOW-INCOME RESIDENT

Studies of residents in economic and class integrated environments are rare; and those that exist have been done on less than a community-wide scale. Because of the dearth of knowledge in the area, many still question the feasibility of socioeconomic integration. For example, the National Academy of Sciences' study of segregation concluded that,

> A more adequate knowledge base is needed in order to determine the feasibility of socioeconomic residential mixing. More information is needed about why people live where they do—specifically, (a) housing preferences and attitudes; (b) "real costs" for different socioeconomic groups; (c) public sector costs and benefits, both perceived and actual; (d) alternative approaches to correcting public sector costs and changing individual "real costs;" and (e) the "human costs" of socioeconomic stratification (Hawley and Rock 1973, p. 20).

The information presented below provides some of the data required to make policy decisions. The costs and benefits from the perspective of the low-income resident are explored and the impact of low-income units on the housing market is evaluated.

Quality of Life

Respondents living in subsidized housing in the new and conventional communities were asked to compare their dwelling unit, neighborhood, community and facilities to their previous place of residence (see Table 7—1). With the exception of one measure— layout and space of dwelling unit—the new community residents of subsidized housing consistently evaluated their present residence more favorably. Although in some instances these low-income residents in the new communities lived further from facilities and services (see Table 4—5), many more felt that facilities were better than those in their previous places of residence. In fact, the low-income residents in the new communities were much closer in their evaluations of facilities and other components of the community to their higher income neighbors than to the respondents who were living in conventional community subsidized housing.

On several important factors—cost of living, finding a job and the type of people living in the neighborhood—fewer than 50 percent of all respondents said that their current locale was "better." However, on all of these measures, the low income residents in the new communities were more positive than those living in the conventional communities; and, in the case of finding a job and the cost of living, they were much more positive than the higher income respondents living in the same communities. While the evaluations of facilities do not appear to be related to propinquity, job opportunity perceptions were based on reality. As indicated in Table 4—6, more new community low-income than high-income residents were employed in the communities where they resided.

More evidence supporting the contention that the quality of life for lower status families in new communities was preferable to that in less planned environments is presented in Table 7—2. Compared to subsidized housing respondents in the conventional communities, new community residents living in subsidized housing gave much higher evaluations of community components and were more satisfied with the impact of the move to the community on their quality of life; almost three times as many said that they would advise friends and relatives to move to the communities.

As shown in Table 7—3, the move to new communities had a more favorable impact on the quality of life of blacks than of whites. Also, more blacks said that they would advise their friends and relatives to move to the communities. It is interesting that blacks had this overall higher assessment of impact on their lives, while their evaluation of individual facilities and services was not always as high as that of whites. It is also evident that new communities provided a better environment for low-income blacks than less planned environments. More than three-fourths of the subsidized housing blacks in the new communities said that the move had improved their quality of life, while 50 percent of those in the conventional communities responded the same way. More striking is the fact that 84 percent of the former and only 24 percent of the latter said that they would encourage their friends and relatives to move to their communities.

Social Integration

As noted in Chapter 2, concern has been expressed over the possible social isolation of lower status persons in a potentially hostile environment. This concern appears to be unwarranted (see Table 7—4). Low-income residents in the new communities do not appear to be at all isolated. They had more interaction with friends and relatives than their higher income neighbors or than the respondents who were living in the conventional communities. They did not differ in their perceptions of whether people were alike in the community. The lower status families also did not see their neighbors as hostile. Sixty-nine percent felt that "it is easier to call on neighbors in time of need" than it was in their previous place of residence.

From the perspective of the lower status person, new communities appear to offer physical, social and economic advantages without the undesirable side-effects many fear. Unfortunately, there was not enough variation in the spatial location of the subsidized housing projects to evaluate the impact of micro- versus macro-integration.

IMPACT OF SUBSIDIZED HOUSING UNITS ON HOUSING MARKET

In their study of new community developers, Eichler and Kaplan (1970, p. 111) found that builders feared, "that the inclusion of lower income families in their development, even in separate subdivisions, would drastically impair sales to the more affluent." As part of their test of this assumption, Eichler and Kaplan utilized the results of the Werthman, Mandel and Dienstfrey (1965) study. From interviews with middle and upper middle class residents in stratified new communities, Werthman, Mandel and Dienstfrey concluded that part of the purpose of planning is to minimize the risk of home investment. In order to do this a developer creates a community with costly amenities and no low-cost housing.

Werthman, Mandel and Dienstfrey's findings are predictable, given the composition of the communities selected for the study. As the data presented in Chapter 6 show, there is a pool of middle and upper middle class consumers who will buy into an economically balanced community. The findings in this study also indicate that in no case has the existence of subsidized units adversely effected the

Table 7-1.   Respondents' Comparisons of Dwelling Unit, Neighborhood, Facilities and Community to Previous Place of Residence *(percent responding "better")*

	New Communities		Subsidized Housing	
Housing and Community Characteristics	*No Subsidized Housing*	*With Subsidized Housing*[a]	*New Communities*	*Conventional Communities*
Dwelling Unit				
Layout and space	69	66	65	66
Construction of the dwelling	45	43	43	41
Cost of buying or renting	38	25	55	49
Neighborhood				
Appearance of immediate neighborhood	65	61	51	47
Facilities and Services				
Public schools	43	46	59	48
Health and medical services	24	25	35	17
Shopping facilities	38	37	42	35
Recreational facilities	61	71	74	27
Community				
Nearness to the outdoors and natural environment	61	68	71	53
Safety from crime	48	47	44	29
Opportunities for participation in community life	60	66	69	45
Good place to raise children	63	70	67	49
Cost of living in the community	17	12	27	18
Finding a job in community	24	28	45	19
Convenience to work	37	42	54	31

Ease of getting around the community	44	55	60	27
Type of people living in the neighborhood	46	48	32	27
Community planning	75	79	78	35
Sample size	1996	883	271	243

[a]Figures do not include responses of residents living in subsidized housing.

Table 7-2. Evaluation of Facilities, Services and Community and Satisfaction with Life Domain Components
(percent of respondents)

Evaluations	New Communities		Subsidized Housing	
	No Subsidized Housing	With Subsidized Housing[a]	New Communities	Conventional Communities
Evaluations (percent rating good or excellent)				
Community as a place to live	89	85	79	46
Health care	66	49	51	35
Recreation	75	83	73	22
Schools	78	76	76	63
Shopping	66	60	56	54
Satisfaction (percent very or completely satisfied)				
Dwelling unit	80	63	40	32
Standard of living	77	64	37	33
With life overall	76	63	54	44
Effect of Move to Community on Quality of Life (percent responding improved)	67	65	68	54
Advice to Relatives and Friends (percent saying community is a particularly good place to which to move)	81	77	71	26
Sample size	1996	883	271	243

[a]Figures do not include responses of residents living in subsidized housing.

Table 7–3. Subsidized Housing Residents' Evaluations of Facilities, Services and Community and Satisfaction with Life Domain Components by Race of Respondent *(percent of respondents)*

	New Communities		Conventional Communities	
Evaluations	*White*	*Black*	*White*	*Black*
Evaluations (percent rating good or excellent)				
Community as a place to live	80	70	53	39
Health care	52	44	44	24
Recreation	75	62	29	13
Schools	77	71	39	61
Shopping	52	78	71	36
Social Integration (percent agreeing)				
People in the community are pretty much the same	56	60	59	60
Easier to call on neighbors in time of need than previous residence	71	57	66	50
Satisfaction (percent very or completely satisfied)				
Dwelling unit	38	50	35	30
Standard of living	36	37	46	21
Overall quality of life	54	50	51	37
Effect of Move to Community on Quality of Life				
(percent responding improved)	66	77	58	50
Advice to Relatives and Friends				
(percent saying community is a particularly good place to which to move)	63	84	27	24
Sample size	222	47	109	122

Table 7-4. Social Integration in Community (percent of respondents)

Indicator	New Communities			Subsidized Housing	
	No Subsidized Housing	With Subsidized Housing[a]		New Communities	Conventional Communities
Most or All of Friends Live in Community	22	22		26	23
Visit with Friends at Least Once a Week	62	67		80	78
Visit with Relatives at Least Once a Week	61	70		75	61
Agree that People Who Live in Community Are Pretty Much the Same	70	55		57	59
Agree that it is Easier to Call on Neighbors in Time of Need than Previous Residence	75	74		69	60
Sample size	1996	878		270	230

[a]Figures do not include responses of residents of subsidized housing.

housing market or property values in any of the communities.[a] This conclusion is based on interviews with builders, realtors and mortgage bankers in each of the areas where the communities are located, and on comparison of home construction rates and sales with surrounding communities.

At the time the data were gathered, of the communities with subsidized housing only Jonathan was experiencing lower than expected growth. The reasons for this were not significantly related to the existence or number of subsidized units. Distance from the beltline surrounding the Minneapolis area, poor access roads and competition from two well planned, more conveniently located, large PUD's appeared to be the causes. It should be noted that both of these competing developments were planning subsidized housing projects.

Securing the investment of property owners in new communities was not a problem. A greater problem seemed to be the ability to control inflated property values. For example, a home purchased for $25,000 in Columbia in 1969 was worth more than $45,000 on the market in 1974. Characteristics of new community development completed infrastructure and amenities—generally operated against any negative impact on the housing market or property values.

CONCLUSIONS

Data to support the desirability and feasibility of socioeconomic integration have been presented. The lower income residents in the new communities were provided a better environment than their previous place of residence or than similar housing in less planned environments. Although these residents of subsidized housing were significantly lower on all socioeconomic status measures than their nonsubsidized housing neighbors, they were not experiencing the negative social effects many predicted. Overall, their quality of life had improved by the move to the new communities.

Another prediction—the adverse impact of low-income housing on the market—appeared not to be supported by the findings. Again, there was difficulty in determining if any potential customers decided not to move to those communities which were integrated.

One of the most important consequences of integration was discussed in the previous chapter—supportive integration attitudes. Residents living in communities with low-cost housing were clearly more favorable toward economic and class integration, and racial integration had the same effect on racial attitudes.

[a]Subsidized housing has been shown not to negatively effect property values in suburban areas. See, for example, Robert Schafer (1972).

Chapter 8

Economic and Class Integration: Policies and Strategies

Unfortunately, the tremendous post-World War II economic growth has not resulted in a redistribution of income to those at the bottom of the economic ladder. The problems of these poor families have been exacerbated by the stratified nature of our metropolitan areas. This stratification creates inequities because,

> The distribution of housing affects the distribution of governmental costs and revenues. It affects the nature and length of the "journey to work," the accessibility of jobs, and the accessibility of the labor force. It determines the degree to which public services and amenities are equitably distributed. And it apparently affects the nature and degree of communication, understanding, and compassion between the different elements of society. It also influences the degree and nature of the "sense of community" (Barton-Aschman Associates Inc. 1971, p. 15).

The poor and most nonwhites have been denied access to communities that provide greater amenities and services and offer a generally better quality of life not only because they cannot afford to live there, but also because of public and private exclusionary policies. In today's housing market, subsidies are the only way in which the poor can move into most suburban areas. And most suburban communities have resisted, through zoning and other mechanisms, pursuing integration policies.

The ideal strategy appears to be the provision of strong incentives to build in communities where there are no perceivable costs to developers or to residents. New communities appear to be a *de novo* method for integration. The rationale for a policy of economic and class integration in new communities is partly based on the premise that they can provide a mechanism for demonstrating that housing for low- and moderate-income families can be designed, grouped and distributed in such ways as to break down middle class hostility to it and to its occupants, while providing a better quality of life for the low-income families.

The findings of this study indicate that many new communities have, in fact, been able to do this, without a negative market impact. Not only is economic, class and racial integration politically and economically feasible, it appears to be beneficial for the low-income families.

The key factor which appears to distinguish between those communities which have implemented class integration policies and those which have not is the developer's perception of the market. In effect, the developer creates the market. If there is a commitment to integration, the data indicate that it can be implemented in almost any area.

Once the decision is made to integrate, implementation is facilitated by informing prospective residents of the goals through honest advertising. Middle and upper class residents of integrated communities support integration policies to a significantly greater extent than their counterparts in segregated ones. This variance is due, in part, to self-selection. More important, however, there appears to be some attitude change occurring by living in a class-mixed community. This finding has important policy implications. If resident support for integration can be attributed only to self-selection, there is a limited pool of potential residents for integrated communities. If attitude change, through contact is occurring, the pool is much larger.

Part of the rationale for the federal new communities legislation was its demonstration potential for integration. However, not everyone was enthusiastic about untested government intervention. For example, Michael Stegman noted,

> One way of measuring the social value of public expenditure in support of new communities that provide adequate housing, employment, and related opportunities for large numbers of low-income and minority households is to strip the new-towns concept of its social objectives and first inquire into the financial feasibility of privately financed, market oriented, large-scale community developments, and then proceed to estimate the public subsidies required to make it financially advantageous for them to pursue variously defined social objectives (1971, p. 336).

This go-slow approach may have some credibility for the overall new community concept in this country. However, as the findings of this study indicate, social objectives can be pursued without damage to the housing market and with positive social impact. To delay implementation policies in new communities or other less-planned suburban communities will only serve to reinforce the inequitable patterns of housing distribution.

Appendixes

Appendix A

Selection of New Communities
and Household Survey Procedures

SELECTION OF SAMPLE COMMUNITIES

The communities studied included fifteen new communities, fifteen paired conventional communities, and three conventional suburban communities with subsidized housing for low- and moderate-income residents.

Selection of the New Communities

The sample of new communities was selected in stages. First, sixty-three new communities and large-scale developments were identified from a list prepared by the New Communities Division of the Department of Housing and Urban Development (1969). The communities on the HUD list were screened against two sets of criteria. First, the communities were evaluated in terms of their conformance to five criteria which are basic to the new community concept:

1. *Unified ownership*—community development under the direction of a single entrepreneur or development company to insure unified and coordinated management of the development process.
2. *Planning*—development programmed in accordance with an overall master plan.
3. *Size*—2000 or more acres planned for an eventual population of 20,000 or more people to allow for social diversity and to support a variety of urban functions.
4. *Self-sufficiency*—provision for a variety of urban functions through the reservation of land for residential, commercial, industrial, public and institutional uses.

5. *Housing choice*—provision of a variety of housing choices, including, at a minimum, opportunities for owning and renting and for single-family and apartment life styles.

The application of these criteria to the communities on the HUD list significantly narrowed the number of projects that were eligible for inclusion in the study. Large-scale land development projects that were excluded from the study at this stage included special purpose communities, such as resort and retirement projects; suburban planned unit developments, which could not meet the size and self-sufficiency criteria; and new towns-in town, which could not meet the size criterion.

Three additional criteria were applied to meet the specific needs of the overall new communities study. These included:

6. *Location*—communities located outside of the contiguous forty-eight states were eliminated in order to limit data collection costs.
7. *Age*—communities that ceased all active development prior to 1960 were eliminated in order to simplify recall problems in case studies of development decisions.
8. *Population*—communities with fewer than 5000 residents on January 1, 1972 were eliminated to insure that communities had enough homes, facilities and services in place to provide an adequate basis for evaluation.

The two screening processes eliminated thirty-six of the sixty-three communities on the HUD list.

From the twenty-seven remaining new communities, thirteen privately developed communities were selected for intensive study. Five new communities were selected because they contained unique features of particular interest to the research team:

1. Columbia, Md.—100 percent sample of stratum: communities with 10 percent or more nonwhite population on January 1, 1972.
2. Irvine, Calif.—100 percent sample of stratum: regional cities with projected populations over 150,000.
3. Lake Havasu City, Ariz.—100 percent sample of stratum: free-standing new communities.
4. Park Forest, Ill.—100 percent sample of stratum: recognized outstanding completed post World War II new community.
5. Reston, Va.—100 percent sample of stratum: recognized outstanding design.

A simple random of sample of eight additional communities was then selected from the twenty-two communities remaining in the sample frame. These included:[a]

6. Elk Grove Village, Ill.
7. Forest Park, Oh.
8. Foster City, Calif.
9. Laguna Niguel, Calif.
10. North Palm Beach, Fla.
11. Sharpstown, Tex.
12. Valencia, Calif.
13. Westlake Village, Calif.

The privately developed new communities selected for study allow adequate coverage of the range of variation in the characteristics of nonfederally assisted new communities now under development in the United States. There is no evidence that the inclusion of a greater number of new communities would have yielded greater variation in community characteristics.

Finally, although both Jonathan, Minn., and Park Forest South, Ill., had fewer than 5000 residents as of January 1, 1972, these two communities were selected to insure the inclusion in the study of new communities that were participating in the federal new communities program. At the time the sample was drawn, the universe of federally assisted new communities included: Flower Mound, Tex.; Jonathan, Minn.; Maumelle, Ark.; Park Forest South, Ill.; Riverton, N.Y.; and St. Charles Communities, Md. Most of these were in the very initial stages of development. Only Jonathan and Park Forest South had enough occupied housing for a baseline evaluation. Because at least two federally assisted new communities were required to avoid the problem of generalizing from a unique case, both were included in the sample.

Selection of the Paired
Conventional Communities

For each of the sample new communities, a less planned conventionally developed area was delineated to serve as a control and basis

[a]After these eight communities were selected, the fourteen communities remaining in the new community sampling frame were: (1) Clear Lake City, Tex.; (2) Coral Springs, Fla.; (3) Diamond Bar, Calif.; (4) Janss/Conejo (Thousand Oaks), Calif.; (5) Lehigh Acres, Fla.; (6) Litchfield Park, Ariz.; (7) Miami Lakes, Fla.; (8) Mission Viejo, Calif.; (9) Montbello, Col.; (10) Montgomery Village, Md.; (11) Northglenn, Col.; (12) Palm Beach Gardens, Fla.; (13) Pikes Peak Park, Col.; and (14) Rancho Bernardo, Calif.

of comparison. The new communities and paired conventional communities were otherwise matched in terms of the age of housing, range of housing costs and location within the metropolitan area. In some cases it was necessary to delineate a set of contiguous subdivisions as a comparison area in order to match more nearly the range of housing costs in the paired new community. An effort was also made to match on the mix of housing types; however, this could not be done consistently because the range of housing types available in new communities was not found regularly in other suburban settings. Where older, established communities were listed as comparison communities, only the tracts or neighborhoods within these communities that matched the new community as to age and price range of housing were included in the universe from which the household sample was selected. However, respondents in such areas were asked about the whole community rather than only the subselected tracts in which they lived in household survey questions that referred to the community as a whole.

The paired conventional communities were chosen on the basis of information gathered during site visits to the market areas of the sample new communities and from consultations with county and municipal planning agencies and local real estate firms, analyses of census tract data, and visual inspection of all areas that met the matching criteria. The sample new communities and their paired conventional communities include:

New Community	*Paired Conventional Community*
(1) Columbia, Md.	Norbeck-Wheaton, Md.
(2) Elk Grove Village, Ill.	Schaumburg, Ill.
(3) Forest Park, Oh.	Sharonville, Oh.
(4) Foster City, Calif.	West San Mateo, Calif.
(5) Irvine, Calif.	Fountain Valley, Calif.
(6) Jonathan, Minn.	Chanhassen, Minn.
(7) Laguna Niguel, Calif.	Dana Point/Capistrano Valley, Calif.
(8) Lake Havasu City, Ariz.	Kingman, Ariz.
(9) North Palm Beach, Fla.	Tequesta, Fla.
(10) Park Forest, Ill.	Lansing, Ill.
(11) Park Forest South, Ill.	Richton Park, Ill.
(12) Reston, Va.	West Springfield, Va.
(13) Sharpstown, Tex.	Southwest Houston, Tex.
(14) Valencia, Calif.	Bouquet Canyon, Calif.
(15) Westlake Village, Calif.	Agoura/Malibu Junction, Calif.

Selection of Subsidized Housing Projects
in Conventional Communities

Three additional communities were selected to serve as controls and as another base of comparison with the responses of new community residents of subsidized housing. These were Laurel, Md., Chicago Heights, Ill., and Richton Park, Ill. In each community federally subsidized housing projects were utilized as sampling frames to select low- and moderate-income households that could be compared to similar groups living in new communities. The primary criterion used in the selection of the special comparison communities was that they be located in the vicinity of the sample new communities. This was done in order to limit regional variation and to facilitate comparisons among the communities. They were selected in much the same manner as the paired conventional communities—on the basis of site visits and consultations with local planning agencies and realtors.

THE HOUSEHOLD SURVEY

Residents living in the new and conventional communities were interviewed during the period from February through May 1973. Portions of the interview schedule that were used for the analyses in this book are reproduced in Appendix D. The number of households interviewed in each community is shown in Table A–1.

Selection of Sample Households
and Respondents

The universe sampled for the household survey included family heads and their spouses living in the sample communities. The sample was selected in such a manner that every head or spouse who had moved into his or her dwelling before January 1, 1973, had a known probability of selection. The method of selecting the household sample was as follows.

Visits were made to each sample community between mid–October 1972, and mid-January 1973, to identify all occupied dwellings on large-scale maps showing lot lines for each community. These maps, with the location and number of occupied dwellings delineated, were used to outline clusters of from five to seven dwelling units. The number of units to be included in a cluster was chosen on the basis of projected field costs, expected response rate, and the number of clusters needed to generate a household sample representative of the sample communities. The eventual analysis of housing clusters was considered in delineating sample clusters. Accordingly, the clusters were outlined so as to include dwellings that faced one

Table A–1. Number of Household Interviews

Communities	Number of Interviews		Subsamples	
	Total	Basic Sample	Subsidized Housing Residents	Black Residents
Total	5104	4883	274	150
Thirteen Nonfederally Assisted New Communities	2969	2619	219	131
Thirteen Paired Conventional Communities	1321	1321	NA	NA
Federally Assisted New Communities and Paired Conventional Communities				
Jonathan, Minn. (NC)	207	152	55	NA
Chanhassen, Minn. (CC)	118	100	NA	NA
Park Forest South, Ill. (NC)	219	200	NA	19
Richton Park, Ill. (CC)	101	101	NA	NA
Two Subsidized Housing Conventional Communities[a] (CC)	187	187	NA	NA
Nonfederally Assisted New Communities and Paired Conventional Communities				
Columbia, Md. (NC)	311	213	61	37
Norbeck-Wheaton, Md. (CC)	123	123	NA	NA
Elk Grove Village, Ill, (NC)	199	199	NA	NA
Schaumburg, Ill. (CC)	102	102	NA	NA

Community			
Forest Park, Oh. (NC)	306	202	53	51
Sharonville, Oh. (CC)	115	115	NA	NA
Foster City, Calif. (NC)	176	176	NA	NA
West San Mateo, Calif. (CC)	112	93	NA	NA
Irvine, Calif. (NC)	202	202	NA	NA
Fountain Valley, Calif. (CC)	102	102	NA	NA
Laguna Niguel, Calif. (NC)	208	208	NA	NA
Dana Point, Calif. (CC)	105	105	NA	NA
Lake Havasu City, Ariz. (NC)	256	209	47	NA
Kingman, Ariz. (CC)	93	93	NA	NA
North Palm Beach, Fla. (NC)	202	202	NA	NA
Tequesta, Fla. (CC)	111	111	NA	NA
Park Forest, Ill. (NC)	216	200	NA	16
Lansing, Ill. (CC)	78	64	NA	NA
Reston, Va. (NC)	282	197	58	27
West Springfield, Va. (CC)	95	95	NA	NA
Sharpstown, Tex. (NC)	203	203	NA	NA
Southwest Houston, Tex. (CC)	108	108	NA	NA
Valencia, Calif. (NC)	202	202	NA	NA
Bouquet Canyon, Calif. (CC)	103	103	NA	NA
Westlake Village, Calif. (NC)	206	206	NA	NA
Agoura/Malibu Junction, Calif. (CC)	107	107	NA	NA

NC = New Community   CC = Conventional Community   NA = Not Applicable

[a]Subsidized housing residents living in Richton Park were also included in analyses reported in this book.

another across a street or common court. Dwellings strung out in a row were rarely defined as clusters.

For apartment buildings where the location of individual dwellings was unknown, the total number of units in the building was divided into a designated number of five-, six- or seven-dwelling clusters. For buildings containing fewer than ten apartments, two or three neighboring buildings were grouped together and clusters were designated for all units in the group. Where the location of apartments within a building was known, it was possible to cluster these units directly as in the procedure described above.

After clusters were defined for a community, a probability sample of clusters was selected. The samples in paired conventional communities that had more than one type of dwelling unit available were stratified by dwelling unit type (single-family detached houses, townhouses or apartments) so that the proportion of selected clusters of each dwelling type approximated the proportions of dwelling unit types found in the paired new community. Overall, the selection of sample clusters was designed to obtain 200 interviews in each of the thirteen nonfederally assisted new communities and two federally assisted new communities, and 100 interviews in each of the paired conventional communities and conventional communities used to obtain interviews with subsidized housing residents.

Subsample of new community households occupying subsidized housing. Five of the sample new communities (Columbia, Forest Park, Jonathan, Lake Havasu City and Reston) had FHA Section 235 (owner) and/or 221(d)3 or 236 (rental) subsidized housing occupied at the time of the sampling process. In each of these communities the sampling frame was divided into two strata, one of subsidized housing units and one of nonsubsidized housing units. Separate random probability cluster samples were drawn from each stratum in the manner described above. Selection of clusters was designed to produce fifty interviews with households occupying subsidized housing and 200 interviews with households occupying nonsubsidized housing, in each of the five communities.

Subsample of new community black households. In each of the five sample new communities known to have more than 100 resident black households (Columbia, Forest Park, Park Forest, Park Forest South and Reston) a special subsample of black households was selected to supplement those falling into the regular cluster samples. Lists suitable for use as sampling frames were not available in all five of the communities. Therefore, sampling frames were constructed by referrals from the random sample respondents. Addresses generated by the referral procedure were listed and duplications were eliminated. The five resulting lists were used as the sample frames from which simple random samples of addresses were drawn, aimed at producing fifty additional interviews with black households in each of the five communities.

It should be noted that because it is a referral sample this subsample of black households does not constitute a random sample representative of the population of black family heads and their spouses in these communities. However, comparison of black subsample respondent characteristics and attitudes with those of black respondents from the random sample in the five communities indicated that the two groups were very similar. See Table A–2.

Designation of the household survey respondent. The prospective respondent was randomly designated as either the head of the family residing at the address or the spouse of the family head for each address in the regular cluster sample, the subsidized housing subsample and the black subsample prior to assignment of addresses to interviewers. The head was designated as the respondent for half of the addresses sampled in each community; the spouse was designated as the respondent for the remaining half. Interviews were allowed only with the designated respondent except where the spouse was designated and there was no spouse of family head living in the household. In such situations the interview was to be taken with the family head. If a household was occupied by more than one family unit, the head or spouse of the head of each family unit was to be interviewed.

These procedures left no freedom to interviewers in the choice of respondents. The dwellings at which interviews were to be taken and the individuals to be interviewed within the dwellings were specified.

Interviewing Methods

Interviewers were instructed to ask questions using the exact wording appearing in the questionnaire. When probing was necessary to obtain full answers to open-end questions, interviewers were to use nondirective probes (such as, "How do you mean?" or "Could you tell me more about that?") to avoid influencing the responses.

When recording responses to open-end questions, interviewers were to write the actual words spoken as nearly as possible and to indicate when they had probed for additional information. Recording of responses to closed-end questions simply required checking the appropriate precoded response in most cases.

Table A-2. Comparison of Responses from Random Sample Blacks and the Nonrandom Black Subsample in Five Sample Communities

Characteristic or Attitude	Percent of Black Respondents from[a]	
	Random Sample	Nonrandom Black Subsample
Number of Persons in Respondent's Household		
One	2.2	2.7
Two	23.7	10.0
Three to five	62.6	70.7
Six or more	11.5	16.7
Number of Children in Respondent's Household		
None	23.5	12.7
One	28.2	24.0
Two	28.3	30.0
Three or more	20.0	33.3
Age of Family Head		
Under 35	50.4	45.0
35–44	32.1	37.6
45–54	14.1	16.1
55 or older	3.5	1.3
Marital Status of Household Head		
Married	89.9	86.7
Widowed	0.1	2.0
Divorced or separated	9.0	6.0
Never married	1.0	5.3
Education of Household Head		
High school graduate or less	39.7	33.6
Some college to college graduate	34.5	33.6
Graduate or professional training	25.9	32.9
Employment Status of Household Head		
Employed	95.8	97.3
Retired	1.3	0.0
Not employed (not retired)	2.8	2.7
Family's Total Income in 1972 (before taxes)		
Under $10,000	13.2	15.6
$10,000–$14,999	23.9	13.6
$15,000–$24,999	42.1	44.9
$25,000 or more	20.8	25.9
Tenure		
Owns or buying	67.3	85.8
Rents	32.1	13.5
Other	0.6	0.7

Table A−2. continued

Characteristic or Attitude	Percent of Black Respondents from[a]	
	Random Sample	Nonrandom Black Subsample
Length of Residence in the Community		
One year or less	47.2	32.4
Two or three years	31.8	30.4
Four or five years	17.2	27.0
Six or more years	3.9	10.1
Rating of Recreational Facilities		
Excellent	35.9	26.8
Good	32.9	36.9
Average	16.6	20.1
Below average or poor	14.5	16.1
Rating of the Community Overall		
Excellent	38.0	31.5
Good	44.6	58.4
Average	15.2	10.1
Below average or poor	2.2	0.0

[a]The responses of blacks falling into the random cluster sample in five sample communities known to have more than 100 resident black households at the time the sample was drawn are shown in the first column; the percentages are based on 95 interviews. Responses from blacks in the nonrandom referral subsamples in the same five communities are shown in the second column; the percentages are based on 150 interviews. The five communities are: Columbia, Md.; Forest Park, Oh.; Park Forest, Ill.; Park Forest South, Ill.; and Reston, Va. To be statistically significant, differences between percents in the table that are around 50 percent need to be at least 14.8 percent; differences between percents around 30 percent or 70 percent need to be at least 13.6 percent; and differences between percents around 10 percent or 90 percent need to be at least 8.9 percent.

In situations where the respondent could not be contacted on the first call at a sample household, interviewers were required to call back at the household up to six times in order to obtain the interview. These call-backs were to be made at different times of day and on different days of the week to maximize the chance of a contact. Addresses at which the designated individuals refused to be interviewed were generally reassigned to a second interviewer who contacted the individuals and attempted to persuade them to be interviewed.

No substitutions for sample households or sample respondents were allowed. The addresses of sample households (including apartment designations) were listed for each cluster, and the proper respondent (head or spouse of head) was designated for each address listed prior to assignment of clusters to interviewers. Interviewers were required to interview the designated individuals at the addresses listed.

Reliability of the Data

Sample surveys, even though properly conducted, are liable to several kinds of errors. These include response errors which arise in the reporting and processing of the data; nonresponse errors, which arise from failure to interview some individuals who were selected in the sample; and, sampling errors, which arise from the choice by chance of individuals for the sample who may make the sample unrepresentative of the population from which it was drawn. Some evaluation of each of these types of error is necessary for the proper interpretation of any estimates from survey data.

Response errors. Such errors include inaccuracies in asking and answering questions in the interview, recording responses, coding the recorded responses and processing the coded data. They can be reduced by thoroughly pretesting field procedures and instruments, training interviewers and coders, and exercising quality controls throughout the data collection, coding and editing phases of the research process.

The questionnaires and field procedures used in the household survey were pretested in the autumn of 1972.[b] Pretesting was carried out in a planned community, Crofton, Md., in the Washington, D.C. metropolitan area, with respondents similar to the populations in the sample. Analysis of pretest interviews resulted in some revisions, such as the rewording of questions to make their meaning more clear to respondents and interviewers.

Interviewer training included a question-by-question review of the household interview instrument, the taking of a practice interview, and discussion of this interview with the interviewer's supervisor. Supervisors reviewed interviewers' work with them throughout the field period.

The coding operation involved two procedures. Responses to closed-end questions were scored directly on the household interview and young adult questionnaire forms which had been printed so that the scored responses could be machine read directly from the forms onto computer tape. Responses to open-end questions were hand coded onto coding forms and key-punched from these forms. Coders

---

[b]The field and coding operations for the household survey were conducted by The Research Triangle Institute, Research Triangle Park, N.C. Members of the research team monitored all phases of these operations.

were trained as to the codes and coding conventions used prior to the beginning of this work. Hand coding was checked by coding 10 percent of the interviews and questionnaires twice and comparing the two codings for discrepancies. Errors found were corrected.

Data tapes were checked for inconsistencies and incorrect codes and indicated corrections were made.

Nonresponse errors. Some proportion of the sample in any survey fails to respond, usually because of refusals or the failure of the interviewers to contact potential respondents despite repeated attempts. In the random sample for the thirty-six communities (including two retirement new communities not utilized in the analyses reported in this book) there were a total of 7626 addresses at which there was an eligible respondent after elimination of those addresses whose occupants had moved in on January 1, 1973, or later, as well as addresses that were vacant, commercial establishments and others at which no one lived permanently. Interviews were obtained with the selected respondent at 5361 of these addresses—an overall response rate of 70.3 percent. Response rates varied somewhat from community to community.

Because response rates were lower than anticipated (80 to 85 percent overall), a study was conducted to assess the extent to which nonrespondents differed systematically from respondents. First, response rates were computed by dwelling unit type and found to differ. Households living in higher density housing were somewhat underrepresented. Since residents in higher density areas tend to have fewer children, for example, and were thought likely to view the community and its facilities from a different perspective than residents of single-family detached homes, interviews in each of the sample communities were weighted to give responses from residents of each of the three dwelling unit types a weight proportional to that of the dwelling unit type in the community's original sample.

In addition, a survey of nonrespondents was conducted to gather basic demographic and attitude data.[c] Analyses of these data in comparison with household survey data revealed no significant differences between respondent and nonrespondent households for eight of thirteen demographic items (including race, income, marital status and employment status). For five of seven community and quality of life rating items there were no significant differences between respondents and nonrespondents (including their overall rating of

---

[c]The nonrespondent follow-up survey, involving telephone interviews and mailback questionnaires, was carried out during February and March of 1974 by Chilton Research Services, Radnor, Pa.

community livability, ratings of schools and recreational facilities and satisfaction with life as a whole). The major differences which occurred between respondent and nonrespondent households included age of household, length of residence and ratings of health care and shopping facilities. Since most differences which occurred could be explained by the length of time which elapsed between the original survey and the nonrespondent follow-up survey, it is estimated that the lower than expected response rates obtained for the original household survey do not bias the study findings.

Sampling errors. If all family heads or their spouses living (as of January 1, 1973) in new communities and conventional communities fitting the inclusion criteria noted earlier had been interviewed, the percentages and other values reported in the text would be population values. Because a sample of persons was interviewed in a sample of communities, the reported statistics are estimates of the population values. Any distribution of individuals selected for a sample will differ by chance somewhat from the population from which it was drawn. If more than one sample were used under the same survey conditions, the estimates from one sample might be larger than the population value for a given variable while the estimate from another sample was smaller. The magnitude of random variability of sample statistics from population values (sampling error) can be calculated for any sample providing it is known exactly how and with what probability the sample was selected.

Sampling errors associated with observed differences in percentages between subgroups (e.g., between individual new communities and their paired conventional communities) indicate the minimum size of a percentage difference required for the difference to be considered statistically significant—i.e., for it to reflect a true difference between the subgroups in the population rather than chance variation because of sampling.

DATA WEIGHTS

Before combing the nonfederally assisted new community and paired conventional community samples to produce estimates presented in this book, cases were weighted by factors that include adjustments for each community's probability of selection and expected number of interviews in the community (200 for new communities, 100 for less planned suburban conventional communities, and fifty for subsidized housing subsample). Cases in the five communities having subsidized housing subsamples (Columbia, Forest Park, Jonathan,

Lake Havasu City and Reston) have also been weighted to adjust for over-sampling of households in subsidized housing in the community. In addition, each case is weighted by the proportion of its dwelling unit type (single-family detached, townhouse/rowhouse, or apartment) in the original sample for its community to adjust for differential response rates among the three dwelling unit types.

Data presented for combined nonfederally assisted new communities and combined paired conventional communities are weighted to make all the adjustments listed above: each community's probability of selection, dwelling unit type, disproportionate selection of subsidized housing and expected number of interviews. Data presented for individual communities exclude the weight for the community's probability of selection. Weights for subsidized housing have been applied only for the five new communities with a subsidized housing subsample and only when data for this sample are presented in combination with those from the basic random sample.

Appendix B

Summary List of Subsidized
Housing in New Communities[a]

Irvine, California
  Number of subsidized housing units: None.
  Minority population: 5 percent.[b]

  Comments: In 1971 The Irvine Company proposed a large FHA
            Section 236 project for the community. It was
            rejected by FHA because of scale and location. A non-
            subsidized project for moderate-income families was
            rejected by the community. The Irvine Company
            settled a racial bias suit in which it was cited for fail-
            ure to comply with Section 804(c) of the Civil Rights
            Act of 1968 (bias in advertising). The settlement
            required $20,000 per year for affirmative marketing
            and use of minority models in all advertisements.

Laguna Niguel, California
  Number of subsidized housing units: None.
  Minority population: 1 percent.

Westlake Village, California
  Number of subsidized units: None.
  Minority population: 3 percent.

[a]As of January 1, 1974.
[b]Minority population estimates based on Household Survey, Spring 1973.

Comments: The developer reached an out-of-court agreement in a racial bias suit similar to that involving The Irvine Company. As part of the settlement, the developer agreed to use minority models in advertisements and to spend $10,000 per year plus agency and consultant fees for affirmative marketing.

Valencia, California
Number of subsidized housing units: None.
Minority population: 3 percent.

Foster City, California
Number of subsidized housing units: None.
Minority population: 7 percent.

Lake Havasu City, Arizona
Number of subsidized housing units: 64.
  Percent of housing units in community: 2.9 percent.
Minority population: 1 percent.

(1)   Name and location: Desert Manor Subdivision (formerly Shoreline). Located north of business district and lake, bounded by Holly Avenue and Hurricane Drive and bisected by Havasupai Boulevard.

Configuration: 64 subsidized housing units comprise approximately 50 percent of a subdivision of similar single-family units. The subdivision is conspicuous by the fact the homes are the only noncustom ones built in the entire community. There have been considerable problems with construction.

Builder: Shoreline Development, Alameda, California.
Year constructed: 1969–70.
Subsidy program: FHA Section 235.
Price of units: $17,000–$21,000.
Minority population: None.

Sharpstown, Texas (Houston)
Number of subsidized housing units: None.
Minority population: 5 percent.

Jonathan, Minnesota^c (Chaska)

Number of subsidized housing units: 148.

Percent of housing units in community: 35.9 percent.

Minority population: 4 percent.

(1) Name and location: *Farmhill Townhouses.* Windmill Court, Millpond Court and Fieldstone Circle. Located in the northwest corner of Village One: bounded by Jonathan Boulevard, Bavaria and Geske roads.

Configuration: 96 townhouse units concentrated on one site; across road from expensive single-family homes.

Sponsor: Jonathan Partners (Limited Partnership—Jonathan Development Corporation and Dreyfus Interstate Development Corporation).

Builder: Dreyfus Interstate Development Corporation.

Year constructed: 1970—71.

Subsidy program: FHA Section 236.

Number of units by type and rent:

Number	Type	Rent
8	1br	$120
50	2br	$148
28	3br	$162

(Utilities included)

4 Rent supplement

Minority population: 3 percent black.

(2) Name and location: *Neighborhood 5.* Located south of Hundermark Road in the southwest corner of Village One.

Configuration: 52 single-family homes comprise the entire neighborhood; isolated from rest of community.

Builder: Dreyfus Interstate Development Corporation.

Year constructed: 1971—72.

Subsidy program: FHA Section 235.

Number of units by type and price:

^cFederally assisted new community.

Number	Type	Price
5	2br (with unfinished basement)	$20,000
50	3br (most with finished basement)	$21,000

Minority population: Unknown.
Comments: The same homes with garages were built on larger lots in Neighborhood 3.

Elk Grove Village, Illinois
Number of subsidized housing units: None.
Minority population: 1 percent.

Park Forest South, Illinois[d]
Number of subsidized housing units: 46.
    Percent of units in community: 3.5 percent.
Minority population: 10 percent.

(1)   Name and location: *Burnham Oaks.* 745 Red Oak Lane. South of Exchange Avenue, across from commercial area.

   Configuration: 59-unit, five-story building in complex of four five-story buildings and several two-story apartment buildings.

Sponsor: New Community Enterprises, Inc.

Year built: 1970−71 (Note: The building had remained empty since it was constructed. It was approved for rent subsidy by the Illinois Housing Development Authority in August 1973.)

Subsidy program: Rents are subsidized through the Illinois Housing Development Authority (78 percent of units under FHA Section 236).

Number of units by type and rent:

		Rent	
Number	Type	FHA Section 236	Market
13	1br	$138.00	$192.00
40	2br	$179.50	$250.00
6	2br/2 bath	$179.50	$250.00

(Electricity included and use of pool and clubhouse.)

[d]Federally assisted new community.

Minority population: Unknown.

Comments: Under its project agreement residential development schedule with HUD, Park Forest South was
to have 500 housing units for low- and moderate-
income families at the end of 1973. A 450-unit
(40 percent of the units subsidized) PUD proposed for the Deer Creek Woods area was
opposed for ecological reasons by a conservation
group in the community. The site was in a
wooded area on a flood plain.

Park Forest, Illinois

Number of subsidized housing units: 354.
Percent of units in community: 4.1 percent.
Minority population: 9 percent.

(1)   Name and location: *Juniper Towers.* 350 Juniper Street,
near Central Park.

Configuration: 106 units in a ten-story building in the
center of the community, near open space,
an elementary school, and other apartments.

Sponsor: Housing Authority of Cook County.
Builder: Telander Brothers, Inc.
Year constructed: 1971.
Subsidy program: FHA Section 231 (housing for the elderly).
Number of units by type and rent:

Number	Type	Rent
106	1br	$36–$75

(Gas and heat included)

Minority population: 1.8 percent black.

(2)   Name and location: *Arbor Trails.* East of Western Avenue,
south of Steger Road.

Configuration: 372-unit PUD. 248 units (66 percent) are
subsidized. Four buildings of six stories
each; 18 buildings of townhouses. Buildings
occupy only 8 percent of a 53-acre site.
Isolated from rest of the community.

Sponsor: Arbor Trails Development (Limited dividend—
headed by Jack Telander, builder).
Builder: Telander Brothers, Inc.

Year constructed: 1972–73.
Subsidy program: Subsidized through Illinois Housing Development Authority with 66 percent of the units under FHA Section 236.
Number of units by type and rent:

		Rent	
Number	Type	FHA Section 236	Market
8	Efficiencies	$124.00	$174.00
96	1br	$143.00	$203.00
187	2br	$184.00	$258.00
80	3br + basement townhouses	$225.00	$313.00

(Gas and heat included)

Minority population: 10 percent black.

Forest Park, Ohio

Number of subsidized housing units: 201.
Percent of units in community: 4.4 percent.
Minority population: 9 percent.

(1)   Name and location: *Forest Ridge Subdivision.* Located in northwest section of community, bounded by Circle Freeway (I–275), Kemper Road and Mill Road.
Configuration: The 201 subsidized housing units comprise an entire subdivision of single-family homes. Isolated from rest of community by physical boundaries.
Builders: Imperial Homes   43 units
Crest Homes   60 units
Virginia   38 units
Ryan Homes   60 units

Year constructed: 1970–71.
Subsidy program: FHA Section 235.
Price: Under $23,000.

Minority population: 10 percent black.
Comments: Some of Imperial's houses were never sold because of poor exterior design. Some were rented, some were not occupied. Ryan Homes

had planned to sell some of their units in the
"model cities" area of Forest Park under FHA
Section 235. The sales were caught in the 1973
federal moratorium on subsidized housing.
On July 10, 1973 the Forest Park Planning
Commission granted conditional-use approval
for a 120-unit project for the elderly sponsored
by the Winton Forest Church Center. The
sponsors applied for a FHA Section 236 subsidy
for their five-acre site.

Columbia, Maryland

Number of subsidized housing units: 532.
Percent of units in community: 6.9 percent.
Minority population: 20 percent.

(1) Name and location: *Interfaith Community Homes.* Five sites:
Ranleagh Court—Swansfield, near Tilbury
Woods Gardens; Roslyn Rise—Twin Rivers
Road, opposite Bryant Gardens; Rideout
Heath—Faulkner Ridge, near Cross Fox
Apartments; Fall River Terrace—Harpers
Farm Road, across from Merion Station;
Waverly Winds—Swansfield.

Configuration: 300 townhouse units—60 on each site. The
five locations are within one mile of each
other in the villages of Harpers Choice and
Wilde Lake.

Sponsor: Interfaith Housing Corporation (nonprofit).
Builder: J.K. Ruff, Inc.
Year constructed: 1968—70.
Subsidy program: FHA Section 221(d)3.
Number of units by type and rent:

Number	Type	Rent
30	1br	$ 92.00
165	2br	$110.00
72	3br	$126.00
33	4br	$136.00

(Utilities not included)

No rent supplement

Minority population: 30 percent black.

(2)   Name and location: *Copperstone Circle.* 5688 Copperstone
                Circle.
     Configuration: 108 apartment units concentrated on one
                site; near Oakland Mills Village Center.
     Sponsor: Copperstone Limited Partnership (Rouse-Wates).
     Builder: Tom Harkins.
     Year constructed: 1971.
     Subsidy program: FHA Section 236.
     Number of units by type and rent:

Number	Type	Rent
18	1br	$115.39
60	2br	$125.88
30	3br	$136.37

(Utilities not included)

22 rent supplement units

Minority population: 48 percent black.

(3)   Name and location: *Abbott House.* 5495 Cedar Lane, Village
                of Harpers Choice.
     Configuration: 100 unit, nine-story high rise; across from
                Village Center.
     Sponsor: Rouse-Wates.
     Builder: Rouse-Wates.
     Year constructed: 1971–72.
     Subsidy program: FHA Section 236.
     Number of units by type and rent:

Number	Type	Rent
7	Efficiencies	$117.00
42	1br	$141.50
51	2br	$165.00

(Utilities included)

20 rent supplement

Minority population: 35 percent black (based on pre-rent-up
                applications).
Comment: Same construction as used in Rouse-Wates Opera-
     tion Breakthrough Project.

(4)   Name and location: *Ryland Homes.* Steven's Forest Neigh-
              borhood of Oakland Mills.
      Configuration: Ten single-family homes scattered in a sub-
                        division of 98 homes.
      Builder: Ryland Group.
      Year constructed: 1970.
      Subsidy program: FHA Section 235.
      Number of units by type and price:

Number	Type	Price
10	3br ranch-style built on a slab	$19,990

Minority population: Unknown.

(5)   Name and location: *Tarleton Townhouses.* Located in Village
              of Oakland Mills.
      Configuration: Twelve townhouse units in a project of 156
                        units. (Note: 34 of the nonsubsidized units
                        have a third floor "piggy-back," rent-
                        controlled apartment attached with an
                        exterior stairway.)
      Builder: Howard Homes (joint venture of Howard Homes
                 and Howard Research and Development Corpora-
                 tion).
      Year constructed: 1970—71.
      Subsidy program: FHA Section 235.
      Number of units by type and price:

Number	Type	Price
12	Townhouses (without the "piggy-back")	$19,500

Minority population: Unknown.
Comments: Rouse-Wates proposal for 160 units in Locust
              Park was caught in the 1973 federal subsidized
              housing moratorium. Funds have since been
              allocated. The Rouse organization felt that it
              would be much more difficult to develop the
              project given prevailing high interest rates.

              In the Village of Owen Brown, Howard Homes
              built 18 less expensive models in the 150-unit
              "Greenleaf" development under a new Maryland

State mortgage program. These units were available to moderate-income families earning between $9200 and $11,000 a year. The Maryland Housing Fund allowed 40-year mortgages at 6 percent interest. The availability of these units was made known to residents of the subsidized rental housing in Columbia.

Reston, Virginia

Number of subsidized housing units: 926.
   Percent of units in community: 11.03 percent.
Minority population: 5 percent.

(1)   Name and location: *Fellowship House.* 11450 North Shore Drive, across from Lake Anne Village Plaza.

Configuration: 138-unit, seven-story high rise, across from Lake Anne Village Plaza.

Sponsor: Fellowship Square Foundation, Inc. (Lutheran Church).

Builder: Schultz Brothers, Inc.

Year constructed: 1970−71.

Subsidy program: FHA Section 202 (housing for the elderly).

Number of units by type and rent:

Number	Type	Rent
31	Efficiencies	$107.00−$110.00
69	Studio	$124.00−$128.00
38	1br	$135.00−$140.00

(Utilities included)

27 rent supplement

Minority population: 2 percent.

Comments: Fellowship House II, a 100-unit addition to Fellowship House, received a feasibility letter from FHA on December 15, 1972. The project has since been held up. The Washington Area Office is currently awaiting word on a request for an extension and increase. FHA felt that Fellowship II would proceed rapidly once approved by the regional office.

(2)   Name and location: *Cedar Ridge.* Beacontree Lane, Lake
              Anne Village.
      Configuration: 198 apartment units in nine buildings con-
                         centrated on one site; somewhat isolated
                         from other housing.
      Sponsor: Cedar Ridge Properties (subsidiary of Gulf-Reston).
      Builder: Schultz Brothers, Inc.
      Year constructed: 1969.
      Subsidy program: FHA Section 221(d)3.
      Number of units by type and rent:

Number	Type	Rent
54	2br (small)	$130.00
36	2br (large)	$136.50
54	3br	$161.00
54	4br	$177.00

      (Gas and electricity included)

      Ten four-bedroom units are public housing
      owned by Fairfax County Redevelopment and
      Housing Authority.

      Minority population: 17 percent black.

(3)   Name and location: *Fox Mill Apartments.* Located in
              Hunters Woods.
      Configuration: 240 units in fourteen three-story buildings,
                         concentrated on one site.
      Sponsor: Walker and Dunlop Inc. and Hans Schultz Con-
                struction (limited partnership).
      Builder: Schultz Brothers, Inc.
      Year constructed: 1972–73.
      Subsidy program: FHA Section 236.
      Number of units by type and rent:

Number	Type	Rent
40	1br	$123.63
85	2br	$149.93
80	3br	$165.72
35	4br	$181.50

      (Utilities included)

21 rent supplement units

Minority population: 20 percent black.

(4)   Name and location: *Laurel Glade.* Located in Hunters Woods.
      Configuration: 200 apartment units in a series of three-story
                        buildings (twelve apartments in each struc-
                        ture); concentrated on one site.
      Sponsor: Conrad Cafritz—Reston Interfaith Housing Corpora-
                tion (joint venture).
      Builder: Shareholders Construction Inc.
      Year constructed: Under construction in 1974.
      Subsidy program: FHA Section 236.
      Number of units by type and rent:

Number	Type	Rent
36	1br	$142.20
94	2br	$172.46
70	3br	$190.60

(5)   Name and location: *"Turnkey."* Located in Hunters Woods.
                        Extreme western boundary of Reston,
                        near Laurel Glade.
      Configuration: 50 garden apartment units on one site.
      Sponsor: Fairfax County Redevelopment and Housing
                Authority.
      Builder: American Better City Development.
      Year constructed: Summer 1973.
      Subsidy program: Turnkey.
      Comments: *Tall Oaks Towers*, a 200-unit project proposed
                 for the elderly, was caught in the federal subsi-
                 dized housing moratorium. Sponsored by
                 Redeemer Housing and Shelter Corporation,
                 Tall Oaks had been planned since 1964. FHA
                 rejected previous proposal; it was then revived
                 over exceptional costs limits. The proposal was
                 returned to the sponsor. The sponsors then ex-
                 plored the possibility of state financing under a
                 new Virginia law.

North Palm Beach, Florida
Number of subsidized housing units: None.
Minority population: 1 percent.

Appendix C

Sample Interview Schedule: Developer's Form A and Attitude Schedule

Community:_____   Interview #_____

Performance Criteria for New Community
Development: Evaluation and Prognosis

PART I: SUBSIDIZED HOUSING

DEVELOPER'S INTERVIEW SCHEDULE

FORM A

Respondent's Name:_____   Date of Interview:_____

Organization:_____   Interviewer:_____

Address:_____   Referred by:_____

_____   Comment:_____

_____   _____

Phone:_____   _____

Position:_____   _____

* * * * * * * * * * *

Hello. I'm from the Center for Urban and Regional Studies at the
University of North Carolina. We are conducting a national study
of new communities. One of the most important aspects of the study
concerns housing for moderate income families. We are especially
interested in the experience and attitudes of persons like yourself
who are leaders in the community. As you answer the following
questions, please keep in mind that no direct quotes will be used
without your permission. However, data gathered will be used in
reports and published as part of this research. Of course you are
not required to participate, but I hope very much that you will and
I think that you will find it interesting.

* * * * * * * * * * *

Center for Urban and Regional Studies
University of North Carolina at Chapel Hill

Spring 1973

In this part of the interview I would like to go into some detail about your decision to provide subsidized housing in (Name of Community) and the contracts you have had with FHA, consultants, the builder, local government officials, citizens and others during the initiation and planning of the project.

1. Before we do that, however, could you give me a brief history of the project so that we can put the rest of the interview in perspective.

2.   What were your original objectives concerning housing for low or moderate income families in (Name of Community)?

_____

_____

_____

_____

_____

_____

3.   What were the main factors you took into consideration in the decision to provide housing for moderate income families in (Name of Community)?

_____

_____

_____

_____

_____

3a.   What were the recommendations of your market analysis concerning moderate income housing?

   [0] Did not do market analysis

_____

_____

_____

_____

3b. What were the economic trade-offs you made?

_____

_____

_____

_____

4. Was there a provision for low or moderate income families in the first master plans for the community?

  ☐ 1 Yes   ☐ 5 No
                                      ↓
  ┌──┐
  │ 4a. When was it first proposed?   │
  │   │
  │   _____   │
  │   │
  │   _____   │
  └──┘

5. Who first proposed that (Name of Community) provide housing for moderate income families?

_____

  5a. Was this person a part of your organization, a consultant, or what?

     ☐ 1 Within Organization (position)_____

     ☐ 2 Consultant (name)_____

              (address)_____

                        _____

     ☐ 3 Other (specify)_____

6. During the initial planning period did you decide on a percentage of
    housing in the community that was to be provided for low and moderate
    income families?

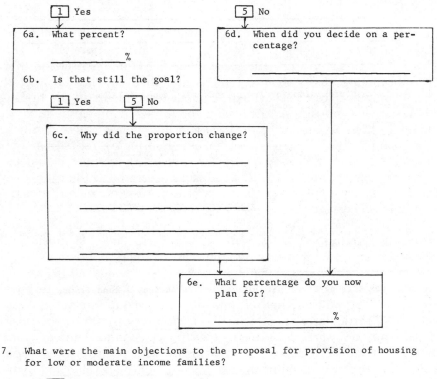

   [1] Yes   [5] No

   ┌─────────────────────────────┐   ┌──────────────────────────────────┐
   │ 6a.   What percent?   │   │ 6d.   When did you decide on a per-│
   │   │   │   centage?   │
   │ _____ %   │   │   │
   │   │   │ _____ │
   │ 6b.   Is that still the goal?│ │   │
   │   │   └──────────────────────────────────┘
   │   [1] Yes   [5] No   │
   └─────────────────────────────┘

      ┌──┐
      │ 6c.   Why did the proportion change?   │
      │   │
      │   _____   │
      │   │
      │   _____   │
      │   │
      │   _____   │
      │   │
      │   _____   │
      │   │
      │   _____   │
      └──┘

         ┌──┐
         │ 6e.   What percentage do you now   │
         │   plan for?   │
         │   │
         │   _____ %   │
         └──┘

7. What were the main objections to the proposal for provision of housing
    for low or moderate income families?

      [0] None ──→ Skip to Question 8

   _____

   _____

   _____

   _____

7a.   Who made the objections?

_____

_____

_____

_____

8.   At what stage of the overall development of (Name of Community) did
you plan to build the moderate income housing?

_____

_____

8a.   Why was that timing decided on?

_____

_____

_____

_____

8b.   Do you now feel that was the right decision?

[1] Yes   [5] No

8c.   Why do you say that?

_____

_____

_____

_____

9. What changes have you made in your plans for moderate income housing?

_____

_____

_____

_____

_____

10. If (Name of Project) did not exist, what would the land have been used for?

_____

_____

_____

_____

_____

_____

_____

_____

_____

_____

_____

_____

_____

11. ☐ IF DEVELOPER SPONSORED PROJECT, <u>GO TO SPONSOR'S INTERVIEW</u>.

12. ☐ IF DEVELOPER IS NOT SPONSOR, CONTINUE WITH QUESTION 13.

13. When did you first have contact with (Name of Sponsor)?

_____

14. Did you contact (Name of Sponsor) concerning the project, or did they come to you with a proposal?

|1| Developer contacted sponsor |5| Sponsor contacted developer

14a. Why did you select (Name of Sponsor)?

_____

_____

_____

_____

_____

14b. What was their initial reaction to your proposal?

_____

_____

_____

_____

_____

14c. What suggestions did they make?

_____

_____

_____

_____

14d. What was your initial reaction to their proposal?

_____

_____

_____

_____

_____

_____

_____

15.   Who selected the group that the project would serve?

[1] Developer   [5] Sponsor

16.   Did you and (Name of Sponsor) agree on the group?

[1] Yes   [5] No

16a.   Why not?

_____

_____

_____

_____

_____

17.   Who selected the site for the project?

[1] Developer   [5] Sponsor

17a.   At what state of the planning did you select the site?

_____

17b.   Were other sites selected before this one was decided on?

[1] Yes   [5] No

17c.   Why were they ruled out?

_____

_____

_____

_____

18. What criteria did you use in deciding upon the site?

   _____

   _____

   _____

   _____

   _____

19. Did you and (Name of Sponsor) agree originally on the cost of the land?

   ☐1 Yes   ☐5 No

   ┌────────────────────────────────────┐
   │ 19a. Why?   │
   │   │
   │   _____   │
   │   _____   │
   │   _____   │
   │   _____   │
   │   _____   │
   └────────────────────────────────────┘

20. Did sponsor purchase the site?

   ☐1 Yes   ☐5 No

   ┌────────────────────────────────────┐
   │ 20a. What was the cost?   │
   │   │
   │ $_____   │
   │   │
   │ 20b. What were the terms of the agreement? │
   │   │
   │   _____   │
   │   _____   │
   │   _____   │
   │   _____   │
   └────────────────────────────────────┘

21. How large a project was proposed -- i.e., how many units?

_____

22. Did you and (Name of Sponsor) agree on the size of the project?

 [1] Yes   [5] No

```
┌─────────────────────────────────────────┐
│ 22a.   Why not?                           │
│                                           │
│        _____      │
│                                           │
│        _____      │
│                                           │
│        _____      │
└─────────────────────────────────────────┘
```

23. How did you determine the size of the project?

_____

_____

_____

_____

24. Who determined the size of the units?

 [1] Sponsor

 [2] Developer

 [3] Builder

 [4] Sponsor and Developer

 [5] Other (specify)_____

25. How was the size of the units determined?

_____

_____

_____

_____

26. What were the main problems you have had in working with (Name of Sponsor)?

_____

_____

_____

_____

_____

27. Do you have a design staff?

         1 Yes   5 No

                            ↓

> 27a. Who handles design issues, such as site
>   design, architecture, etc.?
>
>   Name: _____
>
>   Address: _____
>
>   _____

                     ↓

Skip to Question 31

28. With what design issues, related to (Name of Project) was your design
    staff involved?

		Yes	No	WHO IS RESPONSIBLE?
a.	Site selection	1	5 →	_____
b.	Size of project	1	5 →	_____
c.	Site design	1	5 →	_____
d.	Units' architecutre	1	5 →	_____

29. Did your design staff work with outside designers on (Name of Project)?

    1 Yes   5 No

    29a. Who were they?

          Name:_____

          Address:_____

                  _____

    29b. To whom was this outside group responsible?

          _____

30. Does the design staff have final authority over design issues?

    1 Yes   5 No

    30a. Who does?

          _____

31. During the initial planning of the project did you contact (Name of most local planning agency)?

    ☐1 Yes   ☐5 No ——→ Skip to Question 34

    31a. Why?

    _____

    _____

32. What was their reaction to the proposal?

    _____

    _____

    _____

    _____

    32a. What suggestions did they make?

    _____

    _____

    _____

    _____

33. What were your main problems in working with (Planning Agency)?

    _____

    _____

    _____

    _____

    _____

34. Did you contact any other local governmental agencies? (Not FHA)

     ☐1 Yes   ☐5 No

34a. Who?

      _____

34b. Why did you contact them?

      _____

      _____

      _____

      _____

34c. What was their reaction to the proposal?

      _____

      _____

      _____

34d. What suggestions did they make?

      _____

      _____

      _____

34e. What were the main problems you had in working with
      (Governmental Group)?

      _____

      _____

      _____

35. Did the project require rezoning?

⬛1 Yes   ⬛5 No

35a. Was there any problem in getting site rezoned?

⬛1 Yes   ⬛5 No

35b. What were the problems?

_____
_____
_____
_____
_____

36. What individuals or organizations contacted you about the project?

Name	When did they contact you?	Why did they contact you?

36a._____ _____ _____
                                _____
                                _____

36b._____ _____ _____
                                _____
                                _____

36c._____ _____ _____
                                _____
                                _____

36d._____ _____ _____
                                _____
                                _____

37. Are you satisfied with the manner in which (Name of Management Agent) is operating (Name of Project)?

   ☐1 Yes   ☐5 No

   37a. Why do you say that?

   _____

   _____

   _____

   _____

   _____

   37b. What have been the major problems in working with (Name of Agent)?

   _____

   _____

   _____

   _____

   _____

38. Are there any services which you feel the tenants of (Name of Project) need which are not currently provided?

   ☐1 Yes   ☐5 No

   38a. Are there any plans to provide this?

   _____

   _____

   _____

   _____

39. Of all the individuals, agencies, organizations or others you have had contact with during the planning of (Name of Project) who provided the most help?

_____

_____

_____

_____

_____

40. Who provided the most opposition?

_____

_____

_____

_____

41. What would you say have been the biggest problems in the planning and development of (Name of Project)?

_____

_____

_____

_____

_____

_____

42.   Do you have plans for more subsidized housing in (Name of Community)?

   [1] Yes   [5] No

   ┌───┐
   │ 42a.   What are they?   │
   │   │
   │   _____ │
   │   │
   │   _____ │
   │   │
   │   _____ │
   │   │
   │   _____ │
   └───┘

43.   Has your involvement in (Name of Project) influenced this decision
      concerning future projects?

   [1] Yes   [5] No

   ┌───┐
   │ 43a.   In what way?   │
   │   │
   │   _____ │
   │   │
   │   _____ │
   │   │
   │   _____ │
   │   │
   │   _____ │
   └───┘

44.   Generally, what has been the community's reaction to (Name of Project)?

      _____

      _____

      _____

      _____

      _____

      _____

45. Do you feel that (Name of Project) has been a success?

   1 Yes   5 No

   45a. Why do you say that?

   _____

   _____

   _____

   _____

   _____

46. From the tenants' point of view do you think that (Name of Project) is a good place to live?

   1 Yes   5 No

   46a. Why do you say that?

   _____

   _____

   _____

   _____

   46b. What are their main complaints?

   _____

   _____

   _____

   _____

   _____

47. ☐   ASK QUESTION 48 ONLY IN <u>JONATHAN</u> AND <u>PARK FOREST SOUTH</u>?

47a. ☐   OTHER COMMUNITIES ———→ SKIP TO QUESTION 49.

48.   In your initial application to HUD under the New Communities Act, what proportion of total number of housing units did you propose for moderate income families?

_____

48a.   Was your initial provision for moderate income housing approved by HUD?

[1] Yes   [5] No

48b.   What changes did they ask you to make?

_____

_____

_____

_____

_____

48c.   If your application had been rejected, would you have built subsidized housing in (Name of Community)?

[1] Yes   [5] No

48d.   Why?

_____

_____

_____

_____

49. If you were just beginning development of (Name of Community), would
     consider applying for a loan guarantee or grants under the 1970 New
     Community Development Act?

        ☐1 Yes   ☐5 No

     49a. Why do you say that?

     _____
     _____
     _____
     _____
     _____
     _____

     49b. How much would the requirement for provision of low and moderate
           income housing affect your decision?

     _____
     _____
     _____
     _____
     _____
     _____

                        [GO TO PART II]

Community:_____   Interview No.:_____

In this part of the interview I am interested in your feelings toward housing
types and costs and the social and racial mix of (NAME OF COMMUNITY).

1. First, about what proportion of the housing in (NAME OF COMMUNITY) is
    within the financial means of low and moderate income families (families
    earning less than $10,000 per year)?

    PROPORTION OF HOUSING:_____%

2. Do you feel there is a need for (more) housing for low and moderate income
    families in (NAME OF COMMUNITY)?

    [1] YES   [5] NO

    ┌──┐
    │ 1a. Why do you feel that way?   │
    │   │
    │   _____   │
    │   │
    │   _____   │
    │   │
    │   _____   │
    │   │
    │   _____   │
    └──┘

3. Ideally, what proportion of the housing in (NAME OF COMMUNITY) do you
    think should be provided for low and moderate income families?

    [0] NONE -- GO TO C. 4

    PROPORTION OF HOUSING:_____%

3a. Here is a list of potential housing sponsors. (HAND CARD) I would
    like to know, first, which you think should be involved in providing
    housing for low and moderate income families in (NAME OF COMMUNITY),
    and, second, what their role should be? What about...

	Involvement		Role
	No	Yes	
(1) Developer	5	1 →	_____
(2) Builders	5	1 →	_____
(3) Non-profit groups	5	1 →	_____
(4) Municipality	5	1 →	_____
(5) County	5	1 →	_____

(6) Local/county housing
    authorities   [5]   [1]→ _____

_____

_____

_____

(7) Federal government   [5]   [1]→ _____

_____

_____

_____

(8) Other (Specify)   [5]   [1]→ _____

_____

_____

_____

4. Often a source of concern for residents of suburban communities is the
    price and type of housing units built in their neighborhoods. Considering
    the neighborhoods in (NAME OF COMMUNITY), do you feel that all, most, a
    few, or none of the residents living here (there) would be opposed to
    housing for low and moderate income families within one-half mile of their
    homes?

    [1] ALL   [2] MOST   [3] A FEW   [4] NONE

    4a. Why do you say that?

    _____

    _____

    _____

    _____

    _____

5. Now I would like to go over some reasons people often give when objecting to housing for low and moderate income families and ask your opinion about them. Do you yourself feel that if (more) housing for moderate income families were mixed in neighborhoods in (NAME OF COMMUNITY) with higher priced housing...

	Yes	No
a. Property values would drop?	1	5

Comment:_____

_____

_____

b. Property taxes would increase do to need for increased services?   **1**   **5**

Comment:_____

_____

_____

c. The community would face a drop in stature?   **1**   **5**

Comment:_____

_____

_____

d. The community would become less stable?   **1**   **5**

Comment:_____

_____

_____

e. The people would not fit in with the
rest of the community? ☐1 ☐5

Comment:_____

_____

_____

f. Housing maintenance and condition would
decrease? ☐1 ☐5

Comment:_____

_____

_____

g. There would be an increase in crime? ☐1 ☐5

Comment:_____

_____

_____

h. There would be a change in the character
of shopping facilities because of a need
to cater to the new group's needs? ☐1 ☐5

Comment:_____

_____

_____

i. There would be a drop in the quality of
schools? ☐1 ☐5

Comment:_____

_____

_____

j. Can you think of any other effects housing for moderate income
    families might have?

     [0] NONE

     _____

     _____

     _____

     _____

6. Do you feel there are any positive effects of moderate income housing on
    a community and its residents?

     [1] YES   [5] NO

6a. What are they?

7. If housing for low and moderate income families is to be built in a new
    community, do you feel there is any particular stage in the development
    process when such housing should be introduced?

     [1] YES   [5] NO

7a. When would be the best time?
BEST TIME:_____
7b. Why do you say that?

8. Can you tell me what factors you feel are necessary and what strategies might be used to successfully integrate moderate income families in a community?

    [0] OPPOSED TO HOUSING MIX ON COMMUNITY LEVEL

    _____
    _____
    _____
    _____
    _____

9. What (additional) factors do you feel are necessary or what strategies might be used to successfully integrate moderate income housing into neighborhoods of higher priced housing?

    [0] OPPOSED TO MIX ON NEIGHBORHOOD LEVEL -- GO TO Q. 10

    _____
    _____
    _____
    _____
    _____

10. In addition to the cost of housing, suburban residents are also often concerned with the type of housing which is built in or near their neighborhoods. Again considering the neighborhoods in (NAME OF COMMUNITY), do you think all, most, a few, or none of the residents living here (there) would be opposed to the introduction of higher density housing, such as townhouses or apartments, within one-half mile of their homes?

    [1] ALL   [2] MOST   [3] A FEW   [4] NONE

    10a. Why do you say that?

    _____
    _____
    _____
    _____

11. How about from your own point of view, do you favor mixing different housing types, such as single family detached and townhouses or apartments, in the same residential neighborhoods?

☐1 YES   ☐5 NO

> 11a. Why is that?
> _____
> _____
> _____
> _____

12. Now I would like to turn to the racial composition of (NAME OF COMMUNITY). Can you tell me about what percent of the residents living here (there) are black or members of other minority groups?

PERCENT BLACK:_____ %

OTHER (SPECIFY GROUP)

GROUP:_____   PERCENT:_____ %

GROUP:_____   PERCENT:_____ %

13. Have any efforts been made to bring blacks or members of other minority groups into (NAME OF COMMUNITY)?

☐1 YES   ☐5 NO

> 13a. What were they?
> _____
> _____
> _____
> _____

14.   Should any (additional) efforts be made to racially integrate the community?

| 1 | YES | 5 | NO

14a.   What do you suggest?

_____

_____

_____

_____

_____

_____

_____

14b.   Why not?

_____

_____

_____

_____

_____

_____

_____

15.   Recently, there has been a lot of talk about "fair share" and other proposals for integration of suburbs. What proportion of (NAME OF COMMUNITY)
do you feel should be comprised of blacks or other minorities?

| 0 | OPPOSED TO QUOTAS

_____%

15a.   Why is that?

_____

_____

_____

_____

_____

16. If minorities are encouraged to move into (NAME OF COMMUNITY), how do you expect that proportion to be reached and not surpassed? PROBE FOR "TIPPING POINT" PROBLEMS

    _____
    _____
    _____
    _____
    _____

17. Do you think there is any particular stage in the development of a new community when blacks and other minorities should be encouraged to move in?

    [1] YES   [5] NO

    17a. When would be the best time?

    BEST TIME:_____

    17b. Why do you say that?

    _____
    _____
    _____
    _____

18. What (other) strategies might be used to successfully integrate black and other minority families into previously all-white neighborhoods?

    _____
    _____
    _____
    _____

HAND RESPONDENT CARD
19. More specifically now, I would like to know how you think <u>most</u> of the <u>residents</u> in (NAME OF COMMUNITY) would feel about putting homes for the following types of families in their neighborhoods, i.e., within one-half mile of their homes. Would they think that homes for each type of family would greatly improve, improve, not affect, harm, or greatly harm their neighborhood?

Homes for:	GREATLY IMPROVE	IMPROVE	NOT AFFECT	HARM	GREATLY HARM
a. Retired white families with incomes under $5,000 a year	1	2	3	4	5
b. Retired black families with incomes under $5,000 a year	1	2	3	4	5
c. White families with incomes under $5,000 a year	1	2	3	4	5
d. Black families with incomes under $5,000 a year	1	2	3	4	5
e. White families with incomes of $5,000-$10,000 a year	1	2	3	4	5
f. Black families with incomes of $5,000-$10,000 a year	1	2	3	4	5
g. White families with incomes of $10,000-$15,000 a year	1	2	3	4	5
h. Black families with incomes of $10,000-$15,000 a year	1	2	3	4	5
i. White families with incomes of $15,000 or more a year	1	2	3	4	5
j. Black families with incomes of $15,000 or more a year	1	2	3	4	5

20. Now I would like to know what <u>you</u> think about putting homes for the following types of families in the same neighborhoods, i.e., within one-half
mile, with homes for higher income families. Do you think homes for each
type of family would greatly improve, improve, not affect, harm, or greatly
harm neighborhoods?

Homes for:	GREATLY IMPROVE	IMPROVE	NOT AFFECT	HARM	GREATLY HARM
a. Retired white families with incomes under $5,000 a year	1	2	3	4	5
b. Retired black families with incomes under $5,000 a year	1	2	3	4	5
c. White families with incomes under $5,000 a year	1	2	3	4	5
d. Black families with incomes under $5,000 a year	1	2	3	4	5
e. White families with incomes of $5,000-$10,000 a year	1	2	3	4	5
f. Black families with incomes of $5,000-$10,000 a year	1	2	3	4	5
g. White families with incomes of $10,000-$15,000 a year	1	2	3	4	5
h. Black families with incomes of $10,000-$15,000 a year	1	2	3	4	5
i. White families with incomes of $15,000 or more a year	1	2	3	4	5
j. Black families with incomes of $15,000 or more a year	1	2	3	4	5

21. Next I would like to ask your opinion about individuals and institutions
     which may have helped or hindered the acceptance of low and moderate
     income families and racial minorities in (NAME OF COMMUNITY)? First,
     what about...

   a. The residents of (NAME OF COMMUNITY). Can you think of any ways in
       which their attitudes or behavior have affected the housing or racial
       mix of the community?

       _____

       _____

       _____

       _____

   b. What about (NAME OF NEW COMMUNITY DEVELOPER)?

       _____

       _____

       _____

   c. Local realtors?

       _____

       _____

       _____

   d. Mortgage bankers or other lending institutions?

       _____

       _____

       _____

e. City or county officials?

_____

_____

_____

_____

f. State of federal officials?

_____

_____

_____

_____

g. Exclusionary laws or practices?

_____

_____

_____

_____

Now I would like to ask you some general questions about Federal subsidized housing programs.

22. Generally, how do you feel about the FHA homeownership -- 235 -- mortgage program?

_____

_____

_____

_____

_____

_____

22a.   Why do you say that?

_____

_____

_____

23.   How do you feel about the FHA 236 rental program?

_____

_____

_____

_____

_____

23a.   Why do you say that?

_____

_____

_____

24.   How do you think the federal government's moratorium on subsidized housing will affect the supply of low and moderate income units in this area?

_____

_____

_____

_____

_____

_____

_____

25. Do you think that low or moderate income housing can be built without federal subsidies?

        [1] YES   [5] NO

25a. How can this be accomplished?

_____

_____

_____

_____

_____

_____

<u>BACKGROUND</u>

Finally, I have some general questions about your organization and background.

26.   First, what is the exact title of your position with (NAME OF ORGANIZATION)?

TITLE:_____

27.   In what year did you assume this position?

YEAR:_____

28.   Have you held any other positions with (NAME OF ORGANIZATION)?

| 1 | YES | 5 | NO

28a.   What were these?

_____

28b.   In what year did you first begin working for (NAME OF ORGANIZATION)?

YEAR:_____

29.   In what kinds of housing activities is this organization involved?

| 0 | NONE ———→ SKIP TO Q. 31

_____

_____

_____

29a.   With whom?

_____

_____

_____

30. Besides housing, in what other activities is this organization involved?

 [0] NONE

_____

_____

_____

31. How many employees does this organization have?

_____

 31a. How many in management positions?

_____

 31b. How many are involved in this (these) projects?

_____

32. How many blacks or other racial minorities does (NAME OF ORGANIZATION) employ?

 [0] NONE

_____

 32a. In what positions?

_____

_____

_____

33. How many women does (NAME OF ORGANIZATION) employ?

 [0] NONE

 33a. In what positions?

_____

_____

_____

34. What year was your organization formed?

_____

35. What was the amount of your operating budget last year?

$_____

36. How many years of school have you completed?

> ☐1 0-8 GRADES
>
> ☐2 9-11 GRADES, SOME H.S.
>
> ☐3 9-11 GRADES, PLUS VOCATIONAL
>
> ☐4 12 GRADES, H.S. GRAD
>
> ☐5 12 GRADES PLUS VOACATIONAL
>
> ☐6 13-15 YEARS, SOME COLLEGE

☐7 16 YEARS, COLLEGE GRAD

☐8 17 OR MORE, GRADUATE OR PROFESSIONAL TRAINING

> 36a. What was your highest degree?
>
> ☐1 AB
>
> ☐2 BS
>
> ☐3 MA
>
> ☐4 MPA
>
> ☐5 MCP/MRP
>
> ☐6 LLB
>
> ☐7 PhD
>
> ☐8 Other_____
>
> 36b. What was your major area of study?
>
> _____

37. What is your age?

AGE:_____

38. Do you live in (NAME OF COMMUNITY)?

$\boxed{1}$ YES $\boxed{5}$ NO

38a. In what year did you move to (NAME OF COMMUNITY)?

YEAR:_____

39. How do you feel about (NAME OF COMMUNITY) as a place to live? From your
own point of view, would you rate this area as an excellent place to live,
good, average, below average, or poor?

$\boxed{1}$ EXCELLENT $\boxed{2}$ GOOD $\boxed{3}$ AVERAGE $\boxed{4}$ BELOW AVERAGE $\boxed{5}$ POOR

39a. Why do you say that?

_____

_____

_____

40. What three people or organizations do you feel have the greatest influence
on the decisions that relate to subsidized housing in (NAME OF COMMUNITY)?

40a. Name:_____   Position_____

How does this person/organization   Organization_____
influence decisions?
_____   Address_____

_____   _____

_____

40b. Name:_____   Position_____

How does this person/organization   Organization_____
influence decisions?
                                            Address_____
_____

                                            _____
_____

_____

40c. Name_____   Position_____

How does this person/organization   Organization_____
influence decisions?
                                            Address_____
_____

                                            _____
_____

_____

☐ Ask for copies of any reports or studies which relate to low or
   moderate income housing or racial integration.

☐ Ask for budget reports, annual reports, organizational charts, etc.

THANK YOU VERY MUCH. YOU'VE BEEN MOST HELPFUL.

41. Race of respondent.

   1 White   3 Oriental

   2 Black   4 Other

42. Sex of respondent.

   1 Male

   2 Female

Appendix D

Household Survey Interview
Schedule: Selected Questions

<table>
<tr><td>I.D. NUMBER</td></tr>
</table>

**A NATIONAL STUDY OF
ENVIRONMENTAL PREFERENCES
AND THE QUALITY OF LIFE**
JANUARY – APRIL 1973

OFFICE USE ONLY

Supporting Agency	National Science Foundation Research Applied to National Needs Division of Social Systems and Human Resources Research Grant Number GI-34285
Research Organization	Center for Urban and Regional Studies, University of North Carolina at Chapel Hill	Field Work Subcontractor	Research Triangle Institute Research Triangle Park, North Carolina

A. Sample Cluster Number: _____–_____   B. Sample Line Number: _____

C. Street Address:_____

D. City or Town: _____

E. Respondent Designated on Cluster Listing Sheet: ○ Head   ○ Spouse

F. Hello, I'm _____ representing the Research Triangle Institute, a not-for-profit national research organization and the University of North Carolina. We are conducting a survey about the attitudes, preferences, living conditions, and activities of people in a number of communities across the United States. Since your household falls into our sample in this community, I would like to ask you a few questions. All the answers you give will be strictly confidential and will be used only in statistical tables where your name can in no way be connected with your answers. Of course, no one is required to participate, but I hope very much that you will, and I think you'll find it interesting.

G. Before we start, however, I need to know if you and your family have moved to this address since the first of the year (1973) or if you've been living here longer than that.
    ○ SINCE FIRST OF YEAR - - THANK RESPONDENT AND TERMINATE INTERVIEW
    ○ "LONGER THAN THAT" - - CONTINUE WITH HOUSEHOLD LISTING

H. Time is now: _____

I. Good. Now first, I need some information about the people who live here with you. I don't need the names, just the relationships of the people who live here. Let's start with the adults. What is the age of the head of household? (PAUSE. OBTAIN ALL INFORMATION ABOUT HEAD OF HOUSEHOLD AND CONTINUE WITH OTHER HOUSEHOLD MEMBERS.) Have we missed anyone -- a roomer, someone who lives here but who is away right now?

IF HEAD AND SPOUSE ARE LIVING IN A HOUSEHOLD, INTERVIEW PERSON INDICATED ON CLUSTER LISTING SHEET (AND TRANSFERRED TO ITEM E ABOVE). IF HEAD IS NOT NOW MARRIED, OR SPOUSE IS NOT LIVING IN HOUSEHOLD, INTERVIEW HEAD.

ADULTS

All Persons:
* 21 or Older
  or
* Married, any Age
  or
* Under 21 and
  Living Away From
  Parents

NCS Trans-Optic S388C-321

List All Adults By Relation to the Head	Sex	Age	Marital Status	indicate R "X"
1. Head of Household				
2.				
3.				
4.				

2. Compared to the last community you lived in, would you say that for you yourself, moving to this community has improved the quality of your life, has made it worse, or hasn't made much difference?

① Improved   ⑤ Worse   ③ Not much difference – Go to Q. 3

10. Here is a list of things that people often consider when they move. (HAND CARD B) Thinking of what attracted you to this place, could you tell me which <u>three</u> of these factors were <u>most</u> important in your (family's) decision to move to this community (originally)?

11. Now, I'd like you to compare this community to the one you lived in just before you moved here. For each item on CARD B, please tell me if where you're living now is better, not as good, or about the same as where you lived before.

Yes	No		Better	Same	Not As Good
①	⑤ a.	Layout and space of the dwelling and lot . . . . a.	①	③	⑤
①	⑤ b.	Construction of the place . . . . b.	①	③	⑤
①	⑤ c.	Cost of buying (and financing) or renting the dwelling . . . . . c.	①	③	⑤
①	⑤ d.	Nearness to outdoors and the natural environment . . . . . . d.	①	③	⑤
①	⑤ e.	Appearance of the immediate neighborhood . . . . e.	①	③	⑤
①	⑤ f.	Public Schools. . . . . f.	①	③	⑤
①	⑤ g.	Health and medical services. . . . . g.	①	③	⑤
①	⑤ h.	Shopping facilities . . . . h.	①	③	⑤
①	⑤ i.	Recreational facilities . . . . i.	①	③	⑤
①	⑤ j.	Opportunity for participation in community life . . . . j.	①	③	⑤
①	⑤ k.	Good place to raise children . . . . k.	①	③	⑤
①	⑤ l.	Cost of living in the community . . . . l.	①	③	⑤
①	⑤ m.	Safety from crime . . . . m.	①	③	⑤
①	⑤ n.	Finding a job here in this community . . . . n.	①	③	⑤
①	⑤ o.	Convenience to work; ease of commuting . . . . o.	①	③	⑤
①	⑤ p.	Ease of getting around the community . . . . p.	①	③	⑤
①	⑤ q.	Climate . . . . q.	①	③	⑤
①	⑤ r.	Type of people living in the neighborhood . . . . r.	①	③	⑤
①	⑤ s.	Overall planning that went into the community . . . . s.	①	③	⑤
①	⑤ t.	Other (specify):	t.	①	③	⑤

12. | Response to Question 11r, "Type of people – neighborhood": (MARK AS 11r ANSWERED)
① Better – Continue with Q. 13   ③ Same – Go to Q. 14   ⑤ Not as good – Continue with Q. 13

13. When you said that the "type of people living in the neighborhood" was (better/not as good) what, specifically, did you have in mind? (MARK ALL THAT APPLY)

<u>13a. If better:</u>

Yes	No	
①	⑤	Friendly here
①	⑤	Same race as respondent here
①	⑤	Same age, family life cycle here
①	⑤	Same (better) class, income, education, SES level here
①	⑤	Other (specify): _____

<u>13b. If not as good:</u>

Yes	No	
①	⑤	Not as friendly here
①	⑤	Not same race here
①	⑤	Not same age, family life cycle here
①	⑤	Not same (as good) class, income, education, SES level here
①	⑤	Other (specify): _____

19. I'd like to ask you how you feel now about this area as a place to live -- I mean the area outlined on the map (SHOW MAP). From your own personal point of view, would you rate this area as an excellent place to live, good, average, below average, or poor?

   ① Excellent   ② Good   ③ Average   ④ Below average   ⑤ Poor

24. As a place to raise children under 12, how would you rate this area -- would you say it was excellent, good, average, below average, or poor?

   ① Excellent   ② Good   ③ Average   ④ Below average   ⑤ Poor

25. How do you feel about the places right near your home for children under 12 to play out of doors -- would you say they are excellent, good, average, below average, or poor?

   ① Excellent   ② Good   ③ Average   ④ Below average   ⑤ Poor

   25a. Why do you say that? _____

   _____

   _____

38. All things considered, how would you rate (NAME OF SCHOOL) -- do you think it's excellent, good, average, below average, or poor?

   ① Excellent   ② Good   ③ Average   ④ Below average   ⑤ Poor

48. Overall, how good would you say health care facilities and services are for people who live in this community -- excellent, good, average, below average, or poor?

   ① Excellent   ② Good   ③ Average   ④ Below average   ⑤ Poor

52. Thinking over everything we've mentioned about shopping facilities, overall, how good would you say they are for people who live in this community -- excellent, good, average, below average, or poor?

   ① Excellent   ② Good   ③ Average   ④ Below Average   ⑤ Poor

55. All things considered, how good would you say the recreational facilities in this community and its immediate vicinity are for the people who live here -- excellent, good, average, below average, or poor?

   ① Excellent   ② Good   ③ Average   ④ Below average   ⑤ Poor

60. Sometimes a source of concern for people living in residential areas is the type and the cost of housing going up in their vicinity. If a builder were able to buy up a tract of land within half a mile or so of your home, would you care what kind of housing he built there?

① Yes   ⑤ No -- Go to Q. 61

60a. Would you be opposed to any of the following types of housing being built there? (HAND CARD K; MARK ALL THAT APPLY)

Yes No   ○ Opposed to none   Yes No
①   ⑤ Single family detached homes   ①   ⑤ Garden apartments
①   ⑤ Townhouses or rowhouses   ①   ⑤ High rise apartments

60b. How about the cost of such housing -- would you object if new homes were sold for: (ASK EACH RANGE)

		Would Object	Would Not Object
1) Under $25,000?	1)	①	⑤
2) $25,000 up to $30,000?	2)	①	⑤
3) $30,000 up to $35,000?	3)	①	⑤
4) $35,000 up to $45,000?	4)	①	⑤
5) $45,000 or more?	5)	①	⑤

60c. What if the housing were rental apartments -- would you object if they rented for - - - - -
○ (RESPONDENT VOLUNTEERS THAT HE/SHE OBJECTS TO ALL RENTAL HOUSING REGARDLESS OF COST: MARK HERE AND GO TO Q. 61.)

	Would Object	Would Not Object		Would Object	Would Not Object
1) Under $150/month?	①	⑤	3) $200-$250/month?	①	⑤
2) $150-$200/month?	①	⑤	4) Over $250/month?	①	⑤

63. Since you've been living here, do you think you have been adequately informed about plans for future developments, such as shopping centers, apartment houses and other facilities in the vicinity of your home?
① Yes   ⑤ No

64. What has been the most reliable source for the information that you have gotten? (HAND CARD L)
① Local newspaper   ② Friends/neighbors/family   ③ Radio/TV   ④ Developer

⑤ Community/homeowners' association   ⑥ Other (specify):_____

65. As far as you're concerned, do you think it's a good idea for neighborhoods -- and here I'm thinking of clusters of five or six homes -- to have people of different religious backgrounds or the same religious backgrounds, or doesn't it matter?
① Good if different   ⑤ Good if same   ③ Doesn't matter

66. And as far as you're concerned, do you think it's a good idea for neighborhoods to have people with quite different levels of education or roughly the same levels of education, or doesn't it matter?
① Good if different   ⑤ Good if same   ③ Doesn't matter

67. And do you think it's a good idea for neighborhoods to have people of different racial backgrounds or the same racial background, or doesn't it matter?
① Good if different   ⑤ Good if same   ③ Doesn't matter

68. **Race of Respondent:**   ⑤ Respondent is black -- Go to Q. 71
     (MARK ONE)   ① Respondent is not black -- continue with Q. 69

69. **If a black family moved into this neighborhood, do you think that that would upset all, most, a few, or none of the families already living here?**
④ All   ③ Most   ② A few   ① None

70. **Which of the reasons on this card comes closest to how you would feel about it? (HAND CARD M) Would you:**
(READ CATEGORIES)
① a. wish they hadn't moved in and try to encourage them to leave;
② b. wish they hadn't moved in but try to be nice to them anyway;
③ c. not think about their race very much one way or the other and treat them like any other neighbor; or
④ d. go out of your way to make sure they were made to feel a part of the neighborhood?

72. **Next, would you tell me how many of your five or six closest friends live here in this community -- all of them, most of them, one or two, or none of them?**
④ All   ③ Most   ② One or two   ① None -- Go to Q. 74

73. **How often do you get together with any of these friends -- every day, several times a week, once a week, 2-3 times a month, or once a month or less?**
⑤ Every day   ④ Several times a week   ③ Once a week
② 2-3 times a month   ① Once a month or less

74. **What about your relatives -- how many of the relatives you feel closest to live in this community -- all of them, most of them, one or two, or none of them?**
④ All   ③ Most   ② One or two   ① None -- Go to Q. 76

75. **And how often do you get together with any of these relatives -- every day, several times a week, once a week, 2-3 times a month, or once a month or less?**
⑤ Every day   ④ Several times a week   ③ Once a week
② 2-3 times a month   ① Once a month or less

77. **If a close relative or friend asked you if they should consider moving to this community, would you tell them that this would be a particularly good community to move to, that it's pretty much like other communities around here, or that they could probably do better somewhere else?**
① It's particularly good here   ② It's like other communities   ③ Could probably do better

SELF-ADMINISTERED SECTION

Please indicate for each of the following sentences whether you agree or disagree with it and how much. Do this by placing a mark in the appropriate circle under the sentence.

1. All things considered, the people who live in this community are pretty much the same.
   ① Agree Strongly   ② Agree Somewhat   ③ Disagree Somewhat   ④ Disagree Strongly

5. I am able to see my close friends about as much as I want these days.
   ① Agree Strongly   ② Agree Somewhat   ③ Disagree Somewhat   ④ Disagree Strongly

8. It is harder to call on my neighbors in time of need in this community than where I used to live.
   ① Agree Strongly   ② Agree Somewhat   ③ Disagree Somewhat   ④ Disagree Strongly

29. It is very easy to make new friends in this community.
   ① Agree Strongly   ② Agree Somewhat   ③ Disagree Somewhat   ④ Disagree Strongly

33. There has recently been a great deal of talk about building homes for low and moderate income families in suburban areas. We would like to know what you think about putting homes for the following types of families here in this neighborhood, say within a half mile of your home. Please place a mark in the circle which indicates whether you think homes in this neighborhood for each type of family would greatly improve, improve, not effect, harm, or greatly harm your neighborhood.

Homes for:

	Greatly Improve	Improve	Not Effect	Harm	Greatly Harm
a. Retired white families with incomes under $5000 a year	①	②	③	④	⑤
b. White families with incomes under $6000 a year	①	②	③	④	⑤
c. White families with incomes of $5000-$10,000 a year	①	②	③	④	⑤
d. White families with incomes of $10,000-$15,000 a year	①	②	③	④	⑤
e. White families with incomes of $15,000 or more a year	①	②	③	④	⑤
f. Retired black families with incomes under $5000 a year	①	②	③	④	⑤
g. Black families with incomes under $5000 a year	①	②	③	④	⑤
h. Black families with incomes of $5000-$10,000 a year	①	②	③	④	⑤
i. Black families with incomes of $10,000-$15,000 a year	①	②	③	④	⑤
j. Black families with incomes of $15,000 or more a year	①	②	③	④	⑤

Appendix E

Is Laguna Niguel to Remain a Planned Community?

On August 11, the Architectural Review Board denied a proposal submitted by Kaufman & Broad, Inc., one of the world's largest builders of low cost housing, to build condominium apartments at the front door of the Highlands (on property they purchased for that purpose from the Laguna Niguel Corporation in 1969).

Concerned residents at Laguna Niguel are opposed to this development for the following reasons:

1. The existing site of 33 acres of rolling hills will be virtually leveled.
2. Inadequately proposed parking—one carport per unit (no-garages) and open space parking.
3. Architecture is unimaginative and of inferior quality.
4. The architectural plans designed for a housing development in West Covina do not reflect the character of Laguna Niguel.
5. Buildings are distributed in an environmentally unappealing manner.
6. A market comparison shows similarities to "low-income housing" projects.
7. 91 of the 300 units have no space for side-by-side washers and dryers which may necessitate outside clothes lines.
8. Landscaping of Kaufman & Broad projects has generally been very minimal.
9. Two-story buildings account for 81% of the 57 structures.

10. Less than 20% of the units have bedrooms that can be reached without climbing stairs. A contradiction exists since Kaufman & Broad has stated that the project would have a high appeal to the elderly.
11. An independent survey indicates an estimated population of 270 school age children. Kaufman & Broad estimates 120 children out of 300 families.
12. FHA minimum standards are just barely met in some cases.
13. With the exception of one public street, all streets within the development are little more than "alleyways" and privately maintained since they do not satisfy county standards.
14. Anticipated Kaufman & Broad minimum unit square footage is less than the minimum standard now established in the Highlands.
15. We are concerned further by the possibility of other condominiums being developed in our supposedly planned community.

Appendix F

Metropolitan Council Priority
Areas for Subsidized Housing

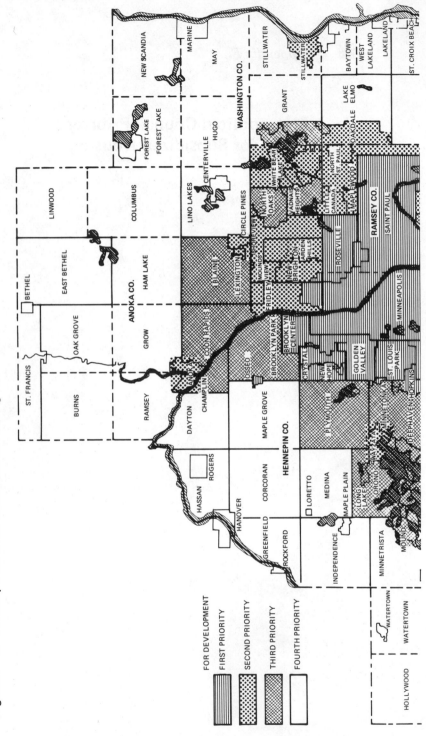

Figure F–1. Priority Areas for Subsidized Housing

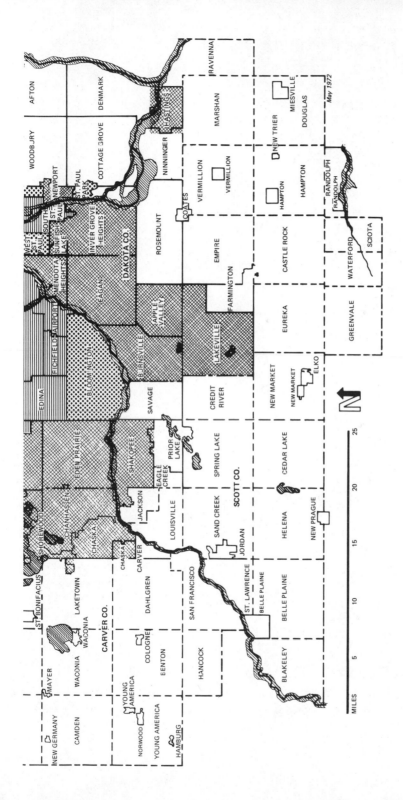

Source: Metropolitan Council of the Twin Cities Area (1972).

Appendix G

Attitudes toward
Socioeconomic Integration

Table G–1. Resident Opposition to Housing for Family Types[a]

Percent Responding That Housing for the Listed Family Types and Yearly Income Levels Would Harm or Greatly Harm Their Neighborhood[b]

New Community	Retired <$5,000		<$5,000		$5,000–$10,000		$10,000–$15,000		$15,000+	
	Whites	Blacks	Whites	Blacks	Whites	Blacks	Whites	Blacks	Whites	Blacks
Jonathan	20	24	32	34	7	9	1	1	1	2
Columbia	15	17	38	40	10	13	2	2	3	2
Reston	24	33	51	54	16	20	3	4	3	3
Park Forest South	34	39	66	71	19	25	1	4	2	4
Park Forest	28	38	69	77	16	31	2	10	3	7
Forest Park	47	57	76	83	25	40	4	19	1	14
Sharpstown	49	63	71	78	30	46	5	22	2	14
Lake Havasu City	38	68	61	81	9	47	5	37	3	32
Foster City	62	67	74	79	44	51	13	17	3	6
Elk Grove Village	50	64	80	84	35	50	4	13	1	8
Irvine	65	72	83	85	48	55	13	25	2	9
Laguna Niguel	63	76	84	86	45	62	15	35	4	24
Westlake Village	68	75	83	89	50	63	19	33	5	18
Valencia	58	70	86	87	45	56	8	19	2	7
North Palm Beach	67	87	84	95	40	75	11	53	5	43
Total	47	57	70	76	30	43	7	20	3	13

[a]*Question:* "There has recently been a great deal of talk about building homes for low and moderate income families in suburban areas. We would like to know what you think about putting homes for the following types of families here in this neighborhood, say within a half mile of your home. Please make a mark in the circle which indicates whether you think homes in this neighborhood for each type of family would greatly improve, improve, not affect, harm, or greatly harm your neighborhood."

[b]Figures do not include responses of residents of subsidized housing.

Appendix H

Effect of Question Sequence on Responses to Neighborhood Mix Items

Table H-1. **Effect of Question Sequence on Responses to Neighborhood Mix Items** *(percent of respondents saying family moving in would "harm" or "greatly harm neighborhood")*

	Questionnaire Sequence First Asked About:	
Family Characteristics	*Black Families*	*White Families*
Black Families		
Retired, income under $5,000	53	43
Income under $5,000	69	68
Income $5,000 to $10,000	42	36
Income $10,000 to $15,000	16	13
Income $15,000 or over	10	9
White Families		
Retired, income under $5,000	49	32
Income under $5,000	67	63
Income $5,000 to $10,000	30	25
Income $10,000 to $15,000	6	2
Income $15,000 or more	2	3
Sample size	2430	2445

Appendix I

Status Concern Index

The status concern index was formed from responses to three self-administered questions:

1. It is worth considerable effort to assure one's self of a good name with important people.
   (1) Agree Strongly   (2) Agree Somewhat   (3) Disagree Somewhat
   (4) Disagree Strongly
2. The raising of one's social position is one of the more important goals in life.
   (1) Agree Strongly   (2) Agree Somewhat   (3) Disagree Somewhat
   (4) Disagree Strongly
3. If a man has an important job, he ought to be very careful about the kind of neighborhood he lives in.
   (1) Agree Strongly   (2) Agree Somewhat   (3) Disagree Somewhat
   (4) Disagree Strongly

Bibliography

Aaron, Henry J. 1972. *Shelters and Subsidies*. Washington, D.C.: The Brookings Institution.

Ahuero, Ceferina, Gil, Vincent, Haskin, Willie Mae, Lilyquist, Marie, and Tong, David. 1971. "New Communities Research." San Francisco: U.S. Department of Housing and Urban Development, Urban Intern Program, San Francisco Regional Office, October 15 (mimeographed).

Allport, Gordon W. 1954. *The Nature of Prejudice*. Reading, Mass.: Addison-Wesley.

Alonso, William. 1969. "What Are New Towns For?" Paper prepared for the Research Conference of the Committee on Urban Economics, Cambridge, Massachusetts, September 11–12.

———. 1970. "The Mirage of New Towns," *The Public Interest*, No. 19 (Spring), pp. 3–17.

Apgar, Mahlon, IV. 1971. "New Business From New Towns?" *Harvard Business Review*, Vol. 49 (January-February), pp. 90–109.

Avco Community Developers, Inc. 1971. *Laguna Niguel General Plan, Amendment #4*. Laguna Niguel, Calif.: Avco Community Developers, Inc., Revised June.

Babcock, Richard F., and Russelman, Fred P. 1963. "Suburban Zoning and the Apartment Boom," *University of Pennsylvania Law Review*, Vol. 3, pp. 1040–1091.

Bachrach, Peter, and Baratz, Morton S. 1962. "The Two Faces of Power," *American Political Science Review*, Vol. 55 (December), pp. 947–952.

Baltimore Regional Planning Council. 1971. *Low- and Lower-Middle Income Housing Production in the Baltimore Region*. Baltimore, Md.: The Council, January.

Barton-Aschman Associates, Inc. 1971. *Orange County, Santa Ana, and Irvine: Recommendations for Making the Development of Irvine a Countywide Success*. Chicago: Barton-Aschman Associates, Inc.

Berry, Brian J.L., and Cohen, Yehoshus S. 1973. "Decentralization of Commerce and Industry: The Restructuring of Metropolitan America," in *The Urbanization of the Suburbs*. Louis H. Masotti and Jeffrey K. Hadden (eds.). Beverly Hills, Calif.: Sage Publications, pp. 431–456.

Bierma, Harry, Jr. 1972. "Review of Housing Market Report: Park Forest South." June 1 (mimeographed).

Birch, David L. 1970. *The Economic Future of City and Suburb*. New York: Committee for Economic Development.

Bradburn, Norman, Sudman, Seymour, and Gockel, Galen L. 1971. *Side by Side: Integrated Neighborhoods in America*. New York: Quadrangle Books.

Brooks, Mary E. 1972. *Lower Income Housing: The Planners' Response*. PAS Report No. 282. Chicago: American Society of Planning Officials.

Brooks, Richard O., and Bordes, John. 1972. "Low and Moderate Income Housing—The New City's Search For A Complete City" (mimeographed).

Bryan, Jack. 1972. "Main Street Revived in Midwest New Town," *Journal of Housing*, Vol. 29 (June 39), pp. 282–289.

Campbell, Angus. 1971. *White Attitudes Toward Black People*. Ann Arbor, Mich.: Institute for Social Research, The University of Michigan.

Campbell, Carlos C. 1970. "New Towns: Metropolitan Decision-Making and Social Implications," in *Planning 1970*. Chicago: American Society of Planning Officials.

Campbell, Donald T. 1971. "Reforms as Experiments," *Urban Affairs Quarterly*, Vol. 7 (December), pp. 133–173.

Clapp, James A. 1971. *New Towns and Urban Policy: Planning Metropolitan Growth*. New York: Dunellen Publishing Company, Inc.

Coleman, James S., *et al.* 1966. *Equality of Educational Opportunity*. Washington, D.C.: U.S. Government Printing Office.

Columbia Park and Recreation Association, Office of Planning and Evaluation. 1974. "A Profile of Columbia Residents Living in Subsidized Housing." Columbia, Md.: The Association, February.

Connolly, Harold X. 1973. "Black Movement into the Suburbs' Suburbs Doubling Their Black Population," *Urban Affairs Quarterly*, Vol. 9 (September), pp. 91–112.

"Corporations as New Master Builders of Cities." 1969. *Progressive Architecture*, Vol. 50 (May), pp. 150–161.

Craig, Lois. 1972. "The Dayton Area's 'Fair Share' Housing Plan Enters the Implementation Phase." *City*, Vol. 6 (January-February), pp. 50–56.

Crain, Robert L., Katz, Elihu, and Rosenthal, Donald B. 1967. *The Politics of Community Conflict*. Indianapolis, Ind.: Bobbs-Merrill Company.

Davidoff, Linda, Davidoff, Paul, and Gold, Neil N. 1970. "Suburban Action: Advocate Planning for an Open Society," *Journal of the American Institute of Planners*, Vol. 36 (January), pp. 12–21.

——. 1972. "The Suburbs Have to Open Their Gates," *New York Times Magazine*, November 7.

Dawson, Paul A. 1973. "On Making Public Policy More Public: The Role of Public Interest Groups." Paper prepared for delivery at the 1973 Annual Meeting of the American Political Science Association, New Orleans, September 4–8.

Deutsch, Morton, and Collins, Mary. 1951. *Interracial Housing*. Minneapolis, Minn.: University of Minnesota Press.

Dobriner, William M. 1963. *Class in Suburbia*. Englewood Cliffs, N.J.: Prentice Hall.

Downs, Anthony. 1970. "Alternative Futures for the American Ghetto," in *Urban Problems and Prospects*. Chicago: Markham Publishing Co., pp. 27–74.

———. 1971. "Residential Segregation: Its Effects on Education," *Educational Digest*, Vol. 36 (April), pp. 12–15.

———. 1973a. *Federal Housing Subsidies: How Are They Working*. Lexington, Mass.: D.C. Heath and Company, Lexington Books.

———. 1973b. *Opening Up the Suburbs*. New Haven, Conn.: Yale University Press.

Duncan, Otis Dudley, Schuman, Howard, and Dunacn, Beverly. 1973. *Social Change in a Metropolitan Community*. New York: Russell Sage Foundation.

Eichler, Edward P., and Kaplan, Marshall. 1970. *The Community Builders*. Berkeley, Calif.: University of California Press.

Elk Grove Village Housing Commission. 1971. "A Progress Report to the Elk Grove Village Board of Trustees." Elk Grove Village, Ill.: The Commission, November 23 (mimeographed).

Farley, Reynolds. 1970. "The Changing Distribution of Negroes within Metropolitan Areas—The Emergence of Black Suburbs," *American Journal of Sociology*, Vol. 75 (January), pp. 512–529.

Fava, Sylvia F. 1970. "The Sociology of New Towns in the U.S.: Balance of Racial and Income Groups." Paper presented at the 1970 AIP Confer-in, Minneapolis/St. Paul, October.

———. 1974. "Blacks in American New Towns: Problems and Prospects." *Sociological Symposium*, No. 12 (Fall), pp. 111–129.

Ford, W. Scott. 1973. "Interracial Public Housing in a Border City: Another Look at the Contact Hypothesis," *American Journal of Sociology*, Vol. 78 (May), pp. 1426–1447.

Form, William H. 1951. "Stratification in Low and Middle Income Housing Areas," *Journal of Social Issues*, Vol. 7, Nos. 1 & 2, pp. 109–131.

Frey, Fredrick W. 1971. "Comment: Issues and Nonissues in the Studies of Power," *American Political Science Review*, Vol. 55 (December), pp. 1081–1101.

Frieden, Bernard J. 1968. "Housing and National Urban Goals: Old Policies and New Facilities," in *The Metropolitan Enigma*. James Q. Wilson (ed.). Cambridge, Mass.: Harvard University Press, pp. 159–204.

Galbraith, John Kenneth. 1958. *The Affluent Society*. New York: New American Library.

———. 1967. *The New Industrial State*. New York: New American Library.

———. 1973. *Economics and the Public Interest*. Boston: Houghton Mifflin Company.

Gans, Herbert J. 1961. "The Balanced Community: Homogeniety or Heterogeneity in Residential Areas," *Journal of the American Institute of Planners*, Vol. 27 (August), pp. 176–184.

———. 1967. *The Levittowners: Ways of Life and Politics in a New Sub-urban Community.* New York: Random House, Vintage Books.

———. 1968. "Planning for the Everyday Life and Problems of Suburban and New Town Residents," in *People and Plans, Essays on Urban Problems and Solutions,* by Herbert J. Gans. New York: Basic Books, pp. 183–201.

———. 1973. "The Possibilities of Class and Racial Integration in American New Towns: A Policy-Oriented Analysis," in *New Towns: Why—And For Whom?* Harvey S. Perloff and Neil C. Sandberg (eds.). New York: Praeger Publishers, pp. 137–158.

General Plan Revision Program, San Mateo County. 1972. *Initial Housing Plan. A General Plan Element.* 1973. Redwood City, Calif.: The County, August.

General Services Administration. 1973. *Acquisition and Occupancy of North American Rockwell Building, Laguna Niguel, California.* Draft Environmental Impact Statement. Washington, D.C.: Public Building Service, Office of Operational Planning, General Services Administration, April 11.

Gladstone, Robert, and Associates. 1964. "Columbia Working Paper No. 22," August 6 (unpublished).

Glazer, Nathan. 1967. "Housing Problems and Housing Policies," *The Public Interest,* No. 7 (Spring), pp. 21–51,

———. 1973. "The Effects of Poor Housing," in *Housing Urban America.* Jon Pynoss, Robert Schafer, and Chester W. Hartman (eds.). Chicago: Aldine Publishing Company, pp. 158–170.

Godschalk, David R. 1973. "New Communities or Company Towns? An Analysis of Resident Participation," in *New Towns: Why—And For Whom?* Harvey S. Perloff and Neil C. Sandberg (eds.). New York: Praeger Publishers, pp. 198–220.

Gold, Neil N. 1972. "The Mismatch of Jobs and Low-Income People in Metropolitan Areas and Its Implications for the Central City Poor," in Commission on Population Growth and the American Future, *Population Distribution and Policy.* Sarah Mills Maxie (ed.). Washington, D.C.: Commission on Population Growth and the American Future.

Goldman, Susan. 1973. "Report of Site and Market Inspection: Hickock Woods (Coop and Rental) Park Forest South." Illinois Housing Development Authority, May 15 (mimeographed).

Goodman, Paul, and Goodman, Percival. 1960. *Communitas.* New York: Vintage Books.

Grier, Eunice, and Grier, George. 1968. "Equality and Beyond: Housing Segregation in the Great Society," in *Urban Planning and Social Policy.* Bernard J. Frieden and Robert Morris (eds.). New York: Basic Books, Inc., pp. 124–147.

Grigsby, William G. 1971. *Housing Markets and Public Policy.* Philadelphia: University of Pennsylvania Press.

Gruen, Nina Jaffe, and Gruen, Claude. 1972. *Low and Moderate Income Housing in the Suburbs, An Analysis of the Dayton Region.* New York: Praeger Publishers.

Hanson, Royce. 1972. *Managing Services for New Communities.* A Report of the Symposium on the Management of New Communities. Held at Columbia,

Maryland, and Reston, Virginia, October 25–28, 1970. Washington, D.C.: The Washington Center for Metropolitan Studies and The New Communities Study Center, Virginia Polytechnic Institute and State University.

Harding, J., Proshanky, H., Kutner, B., and Chein, I. 1969. "Prejudice and Ethnic Relations," in *Handbook of Social Psychology.* G. Lindzey and E. Aronson (eds.). Reading, Mass.: Addison-Wesley, pp. 37–76.

Harrington, Michael. 1965. *The Accidental Century.* Baltimore: Penguin Books.

Harrison, Bennett. 1974. *Urban Economic Development: Suburbanization, Minority Opportunity, and the Condition of the Central City.* Washington, D.C.: The Urban Institute.

Hartman, Chester W. 1973. "The Politics of Housing," in *Housing Urban America.* Jon Pynoss, Robert Schafer, and Chester W. Hartman (eds.). Chicago: Aldine Publishing Company.

Hawley, Amos H. and Rock, Vincent P. (eds.). 1973. *Segregation in Residential Areas.* Papers on Racial and Socioeconomic Factors in Choice of Housing. Washington, D.C.: Division of Behavioral Sciences, National Research Council, National Academy of Sciences.

Heraud, B.J. 1968. "Social Class and the New Towns," *Urban Studies,* Vol. 5 (February), pp. 33–58.

Hermalin, Albert I., and Farley, Reynolds. 1973. "The Potential for Residential Integration in Cities and Suburbs: Implications for Busing Controversy," *American Sociological Review,* Vol. 38, (October), pp. 595–610.

Herrera, Phillip. 1967. "The Instant City," *Fortune,* Vol. 74 (June 1), pp. 135–138.

Hinshaw, Mark L., and Allott, Kathryn J. 1973. "Environmental Preferences of Future Housing Consumers," in *Housing Urban America.* Jon Pynoss, Robert Schafer, and Chester W. Hartman (eds.). Chicago: Aldine Publishing Company, pp. 191–200.

Illinois Housing Development Authority. 1971. *Developers Handbook.* Springfield, Ill.: The Authority, October.

Institute for Urban Studies, University of Houston. 1972. *Housing Market Aggregation: A Pilot Study in the Houston-Galveston Area.* Prepared for Texas Department of Community Affairs. Houston, Tex.: The Institute, April 5.

Institute of Urban Life. 1970. "Estimate of Effective Demand for Low and Moderate Income Housing, O'Hare Airport Area." Report prepared for Leadership Council for Metropolitan Open Communities, June.

Jacobs, Jane. 1961. *The Death and Life of Great American Cities.* New York: Random House.

Jonathan Development Corporation. n.d. *Questions and Answers About Jonathan.* Chaska, Minn.: The Corporation.

Kain, John F. 1968. "Housing Segregation, Negro Unemployment, and Metropolitan Decentralization," *Quarterly Journal of Economics,* Vol. 82 (May), pp. 175–197.

Kain, John F., and Persky, Joseph V. 1969. "Alternatives to the Gilded Ghetto," *The Public Interest,* No. 14 (Winter), pp. 74–87.

Keating, William, D. 1973. *Emerging Patterns of Corporate Entry Into Housing.* Special Report No. 8. Berkeley, Calif.: Center for Real Estate and Urban Economics, University of California, Berkeley.

Keller, Suzanne. 1966. "Social Class in Physical Planning," *International Social Science Journal,* Vol. 18, pp. 494–512.

———. 1973. "Friends and Neighbors in a Planned Community." Paper prepared for the Planned Unit Development Conference, Center for Continuing Education, Rutgers University, New Brunswick, New Jersey, June 4.

Lauber, Daniel. 1973. *Recent Cases in Exclusionary Zoning.* PAS Report No. 293. Chicago: American Society of Planning Officials, June.

Levin, Betsy, Muller, Thomas, and Sandoval, Coranzon. 1973. *The High Cost of Education in Cities.* Washington, D.C.: The Urban Institute.

Lewis, David F. 1974. *A Comparative Analysis of Housing and Resident Characteristics in New Communities and Surrounding Areas.* Preliminary Report. Chapel Hill, N.C.: Center for Urban and Regional Studies, University of North Carolina, May.

Los Angeles Regional Planning Commission. 1972. *Los Angeles County Preliminary Housing Element.* Los Angeles: The Commission, April.

Lowe, Jeanne R. 1969. "Race, Jobs, and Cities: What Business Can Do." *Saturday Review,* January 11.

Marrett, Cora B. 1973. "Social Stratification in Urban Areas," in *Segregation in Residential Areas.* Amos H. Hawley and Vincent P. Rock (eds.). Washington, D.C.: Division of Behavioral Sciences, National Research Council, National Academy of Sciences, pp. 172–188.

Mayer, Albert. 1967. "Greenbelt Towns Revisited, in Search of New Directions for New Towns for America," *Journal of Housing,* Vol. 24 (January), pp. 12–26.

Mayo, E.E. 1972. "Housing Market Data With Conclusions: Will/Monee/Park Forest South, IHDA Market Study for PUD 1–9," May 26 (mimeographed).

Metropolitan Council of the Twin Cities Area. 1972. *Housing Review Manual,* St. Paul, Minn.: The Council.

———. 1972b. *Metropolitan Development Guide: Housing: Policy Plan, Program. December 7, 1972.* St. Paul, Minn.: The Council.

———. 1973a. *Housing: Policy Plan, Program. June, 1973.* St. Paul, Minn.: The Council.

———. 1973b. *Metropolitan Council Staff Report: Subsidized Housing Activity in the Metropolitan Area, July 1972–73.* St. Paul, Minn.: The Council.

Michelson, William. 1974. "Social Insights to Guide the Design of Housing for Low Income Families," in *An Urban World.* Charles Tilly (ed.). Boston: Little, Brown and Company, pp. 421–429.

Molotch, Harvey. 1962. *Managed Integration: Dilemmas of Doing Good in the City.* Berkeley, Calif.: University of California Press.

———. 1969. "Racial Integration in a Transition Community," *American Sociological Review,* Vol. 34 (December), pp. 878–893.

Morrison, Peter A. 1973. "A Demographic Assessment of New Cities and Growth Centers as Population Redistribution Strategies," *Public Policy,* Vol. 21 (Summer), pp. 367–382.

Nader, Ralph, and Green, Mark. 1973. "Owing Your Soul to the Company Store." *New York Review of Books*, November 29.

National Advisors Commission on Civil Disorders. 1968. *Report of the National Advisory Commission on Civil Disorders*. Washington, D.C.: U.S. Government Printing Office.

New Communities Division, Community Resources Development Administration, U.S. Department of Housing and Urban Development. 1969. "Survey and Analysis of Large Developments and New Communities Completed or Under Construction in the United States Since 1947." Washington, D.C.: The Department, February.

Northeastern Illinois Planning Commission. 1973. *Suburban Fact Book*. Chicago, Ill.: The Commission, April.

Orange County General Planning Program, Orange County Planning Department. 1972. *Orange County Progress Report*. Vol. 9. Santa Ana, Calif.: The Department, June.

Orange County Planning Department. 1971. *County of Orange Preliminary Housing Element*. Santa Ana, Calif.: The Department, April.

Orange County Population Growth Policy and Development Strategy Study, Orange County Planning Department. 1972. *People, Policy and Growth*. Santa Ana, Calif.: The Department, December.

"New Housing Options Set for Park Forest South in 1973." 1973. *Park Forest Post*, January 11.

Perloff, Harvey S. 1968. "Common Goals and the Linking of Physical and Social Planning," in *Urban Planning and Social Policy*. Bernard J. Frieden and Robert Morris (eds.). New York: Basic Books, Inc., pp. 346–359.

Peterson, David Lee. 1967. *The Planned Community and the New Investors: Economic and Political Factors in Corporate Real Estate Investment*. Special Report 4, Berkeley, Calif.: The Center for Real Estate and Urban Economics, Institute of Urban and Regional Development, University of California, Berkeley.

Pettigrew, Thomas F. 1973. "Attitudes on Race and Housing: A Social-Psychological View," in *Segregation in Residential Areas*. Amos H. Hawley and Vincent P. Rock (eds.). Washington, D.C.: Division of Behavioral Sciences, National Research Council, National Academy of Sciences, pp. 21–84.

Pinkerton, J.R. 1969. "City-Suburban Residential Patterns by Social Class: A Review of the Literature," *Urban Affairs Quarterly*, Vol. 4 (June), pp. 499–519.

Piven, Frances Fox, and Cloward, Richard A. 1971. *Regulating the Poor*. New York: Pantheon Books.

Potomac Institute. 1968. *Housing Guide to Equal Opportunity*. Washington, D.C.: The Institute.

"Project Agreement Between the United States of America and Jonathan Development Corporation." 1970. October 8.

"Project Agreement Between the United States of America and Park Forest South Development Company." 1971. March 17.

Rabinovitz, Francine F. 1969. *City Politics and Planning*. New York: Atherton.

———. 1975. "Minorities in Suburbs: The Los Angeles Experience," Working Paper No. 31. Cambridge, Mass.: Joint Center for Urban Studies of the Massachusetts Institute of Technology and Harvard University.

Rabinovitz, Francine F., and Lamare, James. 1971. "After Suburbia, What?: The New Communities Movement in Los Angeles," in *Los Angeles: Viability and Prospects for Metropolitan Leadership.* Werner Z. Hirsch (ed.). New York: Praeger Publishers, pp. 133–168.

Rabinovitz, Francine F., and Smookler, Helene V. 1973. "The National Politics and Administration of U.S. New Community Development Legislation," in *New Towns: Why—And For Whom?* Harvey S. Perloff and Neil C. Sandberg (eds.) New York: Praeger Publishers, pp. 93–114.

———. 1975. "A Black Camelot," *New Society,* Vol. 13 (March), pp. 637–638.

Rapkin, Chester. 1969. "Price Discrimination Against Negroes in the Rental Housing Market," in *Race and Poverty: The Economics of Discrimination.* John F. Kain (ed.). Englewood Cliffs, N.J.: Prentice Hall, pp. 112–121.

Rende, Carol Whittaker. 1971. *Far Out! Federal Agency Relocation.* Washington, D.C.: Housing Opportunities Council of Metropolitan Washington, August.

"Report to the Columbia Task Force on a 'Balanced Community' and the Commitment to 10% Subsidized Housing in Columbia, Maryland." 1971. December (mimeographed).

Rodriguez, Filomeno, Jr. 1973. "The Houston Housing Controversy of 1970 Revisited." An Internship Report Presented to the Faculty of the Graduate School, Texas Southern University, August.

Rokeach, Milton and Mezei, L. 1966. "Race and Shared Beliefs as Factors in Social Choice." *Science,* Vol. 151, pp. 167–172.

Roof, W. Clark, and Van Valey, Thomas L. 1972. "Residential Segregation and Social Differentiation in American Urban Areas," *Social Forces,* Vol. 51 (September), pp. 87–90.

Rose, Harold. 1972. "The All Black Town," in *People and Politics in Urban Society.* Harlan Hann (ed.). Beverley Hills, Calif.: Sage Publications, pp. 397–432.

Rubinowitz, Leonard S. 1974. *Low Income Housing: Suburban Strategies.* Cambridge, Mass.: Ballinger Publishing Company.

Ruchelman, Leonard and Brownstein, Charles S. 1973. "Public Need and Private Decisions in Tall Building Development: A Policy-Making Model." Paper prepared for delivery at the 1973 Annual Meeting of the American Political Science Association, New Orleans, September 4–8.

Ryan, William, Sloan, Allan, Seferi, Mania, and Werby, Elaine. 1974. *All In Together.* A Summary Report of the Massachusetts Housing Finance Agency Social Audit. Boston: Massachusetts Housing Finance Agency, January 24.

Schafer, Robert. 1972. "The Effect of BMIR Housing on Property Values." *Land Economics,* Vol. 47 (August), pp. 282–286.

Schnore, Leo. F. 1965. "Social Class Segregation Among Nonwhites in Metropolitan Centers," *Demography,* Vol. 2, pp. 126–133.

Sears, David O., and Kinder, Donald R. 1970. "The Good Life, 'White Racism,' and the Los Angeles Voter." Paper presented at the 50th meeting of the Western Psychological Association, Los Angeles, April 15.

Sears, David O., and McConahay, John B. 1973. *The Politics of Violence: The New Urban Blacks and the Watts Riot*. Boston: Houghton Mifflin Company.

Shaw, David. 1970. "Irvine—City or Super Subdivision." *Los Angeles Times*, June 14. Reprinted in *Basic Issues in Environment*. Ira J. Winn (ed.). Columbus, Oh.: Charles Merrill Publishing Co.

Simpson, George, and Yinger, Milton J. 1973. "Equal Status, Housing Integration, and Racial Prejudice," in *Housing Urban America*. Jon Pynoss, Robert Schafer, and Chester Hartman (eds.). Chicago: Aldine Publishing Company, pp. 147–157.

Smith, Adam. 1937 *The Wealth of Nations*. New York: Modern Library.

Smookler, Helene V. 1975. "Administration Hara-kiri: Implementation of the Urban Growth and New Community Development Act," *The Annals*, Vol. 422 (November), pp. 129–140.

Stegman, Michael A. (ed.). 1970. *Housing and Economics*. Cambridge, Mass.: M.I.T. Press.

Stein, Clarence S. 1966. *Toward New Towns for America*. Introduction by Lewis Mumford, 3rd. ed., rev. Cambridge, Mass.: M.I.T. Press.

Stowe, Eric Lee. 1974. *The Role of Local Government in the New Community Development Process*. Ann Arbor, Mich.: Xerox University Microfilms.

Taeuber, Karl E. 1965. "Residential Segregation," *Scientific American*, Vol. 213 (August), pp. 12–19.

———. 1968. "The Effect of Income Redistribution on Racial Residential Segregation," *Urban Affairs Quarterly*, Vol. 4 (September), pp. 5–14.

Taeuber, Karl E., and Taeuber, Alma F. 1965. *Negroes in Cities*. Chicago: Aldine Publishing Company.

Tenzer, Morton J. 1973. "Businessmen and Urban Politics: The Hartford Process Case." Paper prepared for delivery at the 1973 Annual Meeting of the American Political Science Association, New Orleans, September 4–8.

Toffler, Alvin. 1970. *Future Shock*. New York: Random House.

Twentieth Century Fund Task Force on Governance of New Towns. 1970. *New Towns: Laboratories for Democracy*. New York: The Twentieth Century Fund.

UCI–Project 21 Report on Low Income Housing in Orange County. 1972. *Housing is for Everyone*. Irvine, Calif.: University of California Extension, February.

U.S. Bureau of Census. 1971a. *Current Population Reports*. Series P–23, "Social and Economic Characteristics of the Population in Metro Areas, 1970 and 1960." Washington, D.C.: U.S. Government Printing Office.

———. 1971b. *Statistical Abstract of the United States: 1971* (92nd edition). Washington, D.C.: U.S. Government Printing Office.

———. 1972. County and City Statistical Abstract Supplement. Washington, D.C.: U.S. Government Printing Office.

U.S. Commission on Civil Rights. 1967. *Racial Isolation in the Public Schools*. Washington, D.C.: U.S. Government Printing Office.

U.S. Congress, House of Representatives. Committee on Banking and Currency. 1970. *Oversight Hearings on HUD New Communities Program.* Hearings before the Subcommittee on Housing of the Committee on Banking and Currency, House of Representatives, 93 Congress, First Session, May 30 and 31, 1973. Washington, D.C.: U.S. Government Printing Office.

U.S. Department of Housing and Urban Development. 1972. "Memorandum to Title VII New Community Developers and Interested Parties," from Leonard G. Gordon, Director Applications Review Division, April 20 (mimeographed).

———. 1974. "Remarks Prepared Prepared for Delivery by Alberto F. Trevino, Jr., General Manager, New Communities Administration, U.S. Department of Housing and Urban Development," at the League of New Community Developers, Dallas, Texas, March 8.

U.S. Department of Housing and Urban Development. Office of the Secretary. 1971. "Assistance for New Communities, Notice of Proposed Rule Making." *Federal Register*, Vol. 36, No. 148, July 31.

U.S. Office of Education. 1966. *Equality of Educational Opportunity.* Washington, D.C.: U.S. Government Printing Office.

Ward, Francis. 1975. "Unions Fight Move of Postal Centers to Suburbs as Threat to Minority Jobs," *Los Angeles Times*, March 31.

Watson, Raymond L. 1969. "Statement by Raymond L. Watson, Senior Vice-President of Irvine Company," Statement to a Joint Committee Hearing of the Assembly Committee on Local Government together with the Committee on Urban Affairs and Housing, San Diego, October 30.

Weaver, Robert C. 1964. *The Urban Complex.* New York: Doubleday and Company, Inc.

Weissbourd, Bernard. 1972. "Satellite Communities: Proposal for a New Housing Program," *The Center Magazine*, Vol. 5 (January/February), pp. 7–16.

Welfeld, Irving H. 1970. "Toward a New Housing Policy," *The Public Interest*, No. 15 (Spring), pp. 31–43.

Werthman, Carl, Mandel, Jerry S., and Dienstfrey, Ted. 1965. *Planning and the Purchase Decision: Why People Buy in Planned Communities.* A prepublication of the Community Development Project. Berkeley, Calif.: Institute for Urban and Regional Development, Center for Planning and Development Research, University of California, July.

Whyte, William H. 1964. *The Organization Man.* New York: Simon and Schuster.

Williams, Oliver P., Herman, Harold, Liebman, Charles S., and Dye, Thomas R. 1965. *Suburban Differences and Metropolitan Policies.* Philadelphia: University of Pennsylvania Press.

Wilner, Daniel M., Walkely, Rosabelle P., Cook, S.W. 1955. *Human Relations in Interracial Housing.* Minneapolis: University of Minnesota Press.

Wilner, Daniel, Walkely, Rosabelle P., Pinkerton, Thomas, Tayback, Matthew, and Associates. 1966. *Housing Environment and Family Life.* Baltimore: Johns Hopkins Press.

Wilsey, Ham and Blair. 1961. *Foster City Preliminary General Plan Report.* March 23.

Wilson, James Q. 1967. "A Guide to Reagan Country: The Political Culture of Southern California." *Commentary*, May.

———. 1968. "The Urban Unease: Community vs. City," *The Public Interest*, No. 12 (Summer), pp. 25–39.

Wirt, Frederick M., Walter, Benjamin, Rabinovitz, Francine F., and Hensler, Deborah R. 1972. *On the City's Rim: Politics and Policy in Suburbia.* Lexington, Mass: D.C. Heath and Company, Lexington Books.

Wolf, Eleanor, and Lebaux, Charles N. 1967. "Class and Race in the Changing City: Searching for New Approaches to Old Problems," in *Social Science and the City: A Survey of Urban Research.* Leo F. Schnore (ed.). New York: Sage Publications, pp. 99–129.

Wolfgang, Marvin. 1970. "Urban Crime," in *The Metropolitan Enigma.* James Q. Wilson (ed.). Garden City, N.J.: Anchor Books, pp. 270–311.

Wolfinger, Raymond E. 1971. "Nondecisions and the Study of Local Politics," *American Political Science Review*, Vol. 45 (December), pp. 1063–1080.

Wolman, Harold L., and Thomas, Norman C. 1970. "Black Interests, Black Groups, and Black Influence in the Federal Policy Process: The Case of Housing and Education," *Journal of Politics*, Vol. 32 (November), pp. 875–897.

Wood, Robert C. 1958. *Suburbia: Its People and Their Politics.* Boston: Houghton Mifflin Company.

Zelder, R. 1970. "Residential Segregation: Can Nothing Be Accomplished?" *Urban Affairs Quarterly*, Vol. 6 (March), pp. 265–277.

Index

American Community Builders, Inc., 40
American-Hawaiian Steamship Co., 35, 87
Apgar, Mahlon, 63
Avco Community Developers Inc., 33; in Laguna Niguel, 83

Barton-Aschmar Associates, 123
blacks: attitudes toward economic integration, 109; in central cities, 17; housing opposition as related to income, 99; in media for Columbia, 5; quality of life for in new communities, 114; unplanned integration, 72–76
Brewer, Frank, 36
Brooks, R.O. and Bordes, John, 66

Cabot, Cabot and Forbes, 33
central cities: low-income persons, 14, 16
Centex Construction, 39
Centex Industrial Park, 85, 86
Centex West Inc., 36; opposition to economic class integration, 84
Cincinnati Community Development Corp., 41
Civil Rights Act of 1968, 16, 20; and Westlake Village, 88
class integration: attitudes and individual attributes, 107; difficulty of, 99; existence of subsidized housing, 101; in Gans, 47; and new communities,

28; renters and owners, 105. See *integration*.
Columbia, Maryland, 2; geographic/political climate, 91; housing diversity, 51; integration strategy and marketing, 66–70; market value, 90; nonexclusionary ethos of Rouse, 5; nonwhites/subsidized housing, 48; overview, 41; resident recruitment, 90; subsidized housing, 3, 4
Columbia Economic Model, 67
Connecticut General Life Insurance Co., 41

developers: market decisions and public interest, 89; "new breed," 63; perception of the market, 64, 65; private corporations, 28; profit motive, 7
dispersal: concept of, 14; low-income resident, 19; proximity and attitude change, 101; strategy for new communities, 25
Dreyfus Interstate Development Corp., 73

economic integration: demographics of area, 64; Forest Park, 41; and new communities, 2; perspectives on class mix, 19; state/local barriers, 21. See *integration*.
Eichler, E.P. and Kaplan, Marshal, 63, 70, 89, 115
elderly: lack of opposition toward, 99;

✳

About the Author

Helene V. Smookler is assistant professor of political science at Claremont Men's College and Director of the Rose Institute of State and Local Government. Dr. Smookler was a research associate with the NSF/RANN New Communities Project. She received her Ph.D. in Political Science from the University of California, Los Angeles, and previously taught at Wellesley College, Wellesley, Massachusetts. She is a contributing author to *New Towns: Why—And for Whom?* and *New Communities U.S.A.*, and has published articles on new communities, class and racial integration, and policy implementation.